Sensational

Smoothies

W9-BAG-987

Also by JoAnna M. Lund:

The Healthy Exchanges Cookbook
HELP: The Healthy Exchanges Lifetime Plan
Cooking Healthy with a Man in Mind
Cooking Healthy with the Kids in Mind
Dessert Every Night!
Diabetic Desserts
Make a Joyful Table
Cooking Healthy Across America
A Potful of Recipes
Another Potful of Recipes
The Open Road Cookbook
The Diabetic's Healthy Exchanges Cookbook
The Strong Bones Healthy Exchanges Cookbook
The Arthritis Healthy Exchanges Cookbook
The Heart Smart Healthy Exchanges Cookbook
The Cancer Recovery Healthy Exchanges Cookbook
The Best of Healthy Exchanges Food Newsletter '92 Cookbook
String of Pearls

Most Perigee Books are available at special quantity discounts for bulk purchases for sales promotions, premiums, fund-raising or educational use. Special books, or book excerpts, can also be created to fit specific needs.

For details, write: Special Markets, The Berkley Publishing Group, 375 Hudson Street, New York, New York 10014.

Sensational

Smoothies

A HEALTHY EXCHANGES® COOKBOOK

JoAnna M. Lund

with
Barbara Alpert

A Perigee Book

Before using the recipes and advice in this book, consult your physician or healthcare provider to be sure they are appropriate for you. The information in this book is not intended to take the place of any medical advice. It reflects the author's experiences, studies, research, and opinions regarding a healthy lifestyle. All material included in this publication is believed to be accurate. The publisher assumes no responsibility for any health, welfare, or subsequent damage that might be incurred from use of these materials.

A Perigee Book
Published by The Berkley Publishing Group
A division of Penguin Group (USA) Inc.
375 Hudson Street
New York, New York 10014

Copyright © 2003 by Healthy Exchanges, Inc.
Diabetic Exchanges calculated by Rose Hoenig, R.D., L.D.
Cover design by Ben Gibson

All rights reserved. This book, or parts thereof, may not be reproduced in any form without permission. The scanning, uploading, and distribution of this book via the Internet or via any other means without the permission of the publisher is illegal and punishable by law. Please purchase only authorized electronic editions, and do not participate in or encourage electronic piracy of copyrighted materials. Your support of the author's rights is appreciated.

For more information about Healthy Exchanges, contact:
Healthy Exchanges, Inc.
P.O. Box 80
DeWitt, Iowa 52742-0080
(563) 659-8234
Fax: (563) 659-2126
Email: HealthyJo@aol.com
www.HealthyExchanges.com

Perigee special sales edition: July 2003

This book has been cataloged by the Library of Congress

Printed in the United States of America

10 9 8 7 6 5 4

Once again, my newest cookbook is dedicated in loving memory to my parents, Jerome and Agnes McAndrews. I grew up in the 50s—when girls weren't often encouraged to "spread their wings," especially in rural Iowa! Thankfully, both Mom and Daddy taught my two sisters and me to be resourceful and think through our problems. With Mom's artistic talents and Daddy's analytical skills, I've done just that in this collection of smoothie recipes. By "blending" their abilities, I've created many new and different ways to savor a soothing, yet healthy, smoothie.

As prolific as I am with recipes, Mom was just as fruitful with poems. She dearly loved putting her thoughts on paper and in rhyme. My hope is that both my smoothie recipes and Mom's words bring you pleasure.

First and Last

Although the beauty of a flower fades away,
    its fragrance never really dies.
It leaves a trailing scent of heady perfume on earth
    while gently ascending to the skies.

The prismatic colors and hues in the rainbow
    are objects of beauty to behold.
But the real splendor is waiting at the end,
    stored in a Heavenly pot of gold.

Springtime, with all of her graceful eloquence,
    wearing tinted blossoms in her hair.
First had to awaken from the deep Winter's sleep
    that preserved her delicate beauty fair.

The sunrise, while unveiling its brilliancy,
    is a masterpiece no artist can repeat.
But as long as the dark of night prevails,
    the picture is never complete.

Life, too, has so much ecstasy and charm
    here on Earth's temporary mortal land.
Yet, nothing will compare with the pleasure and joy
    when we finally feel the touch of His hand.
                    —*Agnes Carrington McAndrews*

Contents

Acknowledgments

I dearly love making and drinking Smoothies and I love the following people who helped me to "smooth out the wrinkles" on this "Smoothie Project."

Phyllis Bickford, Rita Ahlers, Gina Griep, and Shirley Morrow—for helping me blend and taste all these recipes. You should have seen my kitchen when every counter was filled with ingredients, blenders, and smoothie machines!

Barbara Alpert—for helping me put my words on paper as clear as they were in my mind. It doesn't matter how good a recipe tastes, if the book isn't written correctly, it could cause cooking disasters!

John Duff and Coleen O'Shea—for helping me take my idea for this book and turning it into a reality. Ideas are only as good as the people helping you!

Cliff Lund—for helping me realize the potential of my dreams. When I often share with him that I have yet another idea for a cookbook, his first question is, "When do I get to start taste testing them for you!?!"

God—for helping me help others with my "common folk" healthy recipes. When I changed my prayer from what I wanted to what I needed, He blessed me in ways I still can't comprehend!

Sensational
Smoothies

Smoothing Your Path to a Happy, Healthy Life

I haven't written very many full-length, "single-subject" cookbooks, but when the idea of doing one on smoothies came up, I knew right away that I wanted to create my own guide to this wildly popular culinary craze!

There are other smoothie books available, full of delicious-sounding recipes, but while many of them emphasize low fat or high fiber, few provide recipes that are reasonably low in carbohydrates—the kind of recipes many people require for good health. That group includes people with diabetes and those with weight loss concerns, as well as others who want to limit the amount of carbs in their daily menus.

That was my principal nutritional goal when I set out to create the 200 recipes in this volume. But of course I wanted my smoothies to be so much more than simply nutritious and low in carbs. My recipes had to be utterly delicious, call for no unusual ingredients, be simple to make, and turn out perfectly when prepared in the most basic blender available. (I know that not everyone has or even desires a $100-plus "blender-to-the-stars"!)

What Is a Smoothie?

What people now refer to as smoothies began life around the time of the first blender, when some enterprising homemaker thought of making a milkshake at home with her engagement or wedding gift blender. She probably noticed a few bits of leftover fruit in her icebox or refrigerator and thought, "Hmm, that might be tasty." Voilà, a fad was born, though it's gone in and out of fashion over the years.

These days, you can't enter a suburban mall or walk down a city street without spotting a store that sells these fruit and dairy shakes. They may use extra ingredients like protein powders and mysterious herbs from the Far East, but the basics are the same as always: a liquid (usually juice or milk) and added ingredients (fresh fruit, yogurt, and other natural flavorings). Some even incorporate vegetables into their blends, especially carrots, which add their own natural sweetness to the mix.

Why are smoothies so popular right now? Well, I believe it has something to do with our fast-paced lives, our desire for good health and longevity, and the appeal of joining fresh ingredients to technology. Smoothies are easy to fix, perfect for eating/drinking on the run, and when prepared well, they're delicious.

Many of the tastiest versions, alas, are also very high in calories and carbohydrates. That fact is often ignored by people who point out that smoothies are low in fat and high in fiber. In fact, many of those who drink smoothies nearly every day for a snack can't understand why they're struggling with weight gain. They might be distressed to learn their "healthy" snacks contain 500 or more calories!

Smoothies We Can All Enjoy

This book celebrates all the joys of the smoothie but also lets you enjoy the treat without the guilt or fear. These recipes deliver all that irresistible flavor and luscious texture, but avoid the high-calorie-and-carb-trap that has disappointed and defeated so many smoothie lovers in the past.

Each recipe has only a few ingredients, all of them available in any small town or rural setting. My hometown, DeWitt, Iowa, population 4,500 or so, is my research lab. If you can't buy it at one of our two supermarkets, it doesn't go into my recipes. Every recipe has been tested and retested in order to deliver the best "bang for the buck," nutrition-wise.

Better still, these smoothies deliver an energy boost in every glassful, and they're simple enough for teenagers to prepare for the entire household. Even younger children can help make smoothies, as long as someone older supervises the cutting and blending.

Don't Settle for Less than Smooth Sailing Ahead

We all live such busy lives, it's not unreasonable to look for short-cuts when it comes to making meals and snacks for ourselves and our families. Smoothies are simple where it counts, delicious without being too decadent, and ready in minutes. What could be wrong with that?

I like to think of smoothies as a kind of symbol for the life I want to lead these days. I don't need to conquer every obstacle that life places in my path; I don't have to volunteer for every community cause, every worthwhile benefit. I've known plenty of bumpy times in the past, and I'm sure I'll experience plenty of potholes in the road I take toward the future and tomorrow.

But for now, I wish you smooth sailing, gentle winds at your back, and a philosophy of life that says easy isn't a "cop-out"—it's a smart choice. I've always made a point of creating recipes using healthy convenience foods. I don't need the "extra credit" some people may believe you earn by cooking and baking everything from scratch.

Living a good life, and celebrating good health, mean making time for what's important. I hope that adding this abundant collection of smoothies to your kitchen shelf will help you make time for all of life's most precious pleasures: time with family and friends, time to pursue new skills and art projects, time just to sit and enjoy the sunset from your back porch or office window.

Food Exchanges and Weight Loss Choices™

If you've ever been on one of the national weight-loss programs like Weight Watchers or Diet Center, you've already been introduced to the concept of measured portions of different food groups that make up your daily food plan. If you are not familiar with such a system of weight-loss choices or exchanges, here's a brief explanation. (If you want or need more detailed information, you can write to the American Dietetic Association or the American Diabetes Association for comprehensive explanations.)

The idea of food exchanges is to divide foods into basic food groups. The foods in each group are measured in servings that have comparable values. These groups include Proteins/Meats, Breads/Starches, Vegetables, Fats, Fruits, Fat-Free Milk, Free Foods, and Optional Calories.

Each choice or exchange included in a particular group has about the same number of calories and a similar carbohydrate, protein, and fat content as the other foods in that group. Because any food on a particular list can be "exchanged" for any other food in that group, it makes sense to call the food groups *exchanges* or *choices*.

I like to think we are also "exchanging" bad habits and food choices for good ones!

By using Weight Loss Choices, or exchanges, you can choose from a variety of foods without having to calculate the nutrient value of each one. This makes it easier to include a wide variety of foods in your daily menus and gives you the opportunity to tailor your choices to your unique appetite.

If you want to lose weight, you should consult your physician or other weight-control expert regarding the number of servings that would be best for you from each food group. Since men generally require more calories than women, and since the requirements for growing children and teenagers differ from those of adults, the right number of exchanges for any one person is a personal decision.

I have included a suggested plan of weight-loss choices in the pages following the exchange lists. It's the program I used to lose 130 pounds, and it's the one I still follow today.

(If you are a diabetic or have been diagnosed with heart problems, it is best to meet with your physician before using this or any other food program or recipe collection.)

Food Group Weight Loss Choices™ Exchanges

Not all food group exchanges are alike. The ones that follow are for anyone who's interested in weight loss or maintenance. If you are a diabetic, you should check with your health-care provider or dietitian to get the information you need to help you plan your diet. Diabetic exchanges are calculated by the American Diabetic Association, and information about them is provided in *The Diabetic's Healthy Exchanges Cookbook* (Perigee Books).

Every Healthy Exchanges recipe provides calculations in three ways:

- Weight Loss Choices/Exchanges

- Calories, Fat, Protein, Carbohydrates, and Fiber in grams, and Sodium and Calcium in milligrams

- Diabetic Exchanges calculated for me by a registered dietitian

Healthy Exchanges recipes can help you eat well and recover your health, whatever your health concerns may be. Please take a few minutes to review the exchange lists and the suggestions that follow on how to count them. You have lots of great eating in store for you!

Proteins

Meat, poultry, seafood, eggs, cheese, and legumes. One exchange of Protein is approximately 60 calories. Examples of one Protein choice or exchange:

> 1 ounce cooked weight of lean meat, poultry, or seafood
> 2 ounces white fish
> 1½ ounces 97% fat-free ham
> 1 egg (limit to no more than 4 per week)
> ¼ cup egg substitute
> 3 egg whites
> ¾ ounce reduced-fat cheese
> ½ cup fat-free cottage cheese
> 2 ounces cooked or ¾ ounce uncooked dry beans
> 1 tablespoon peanut butter (also count 1 fat exchange)

Breads

Breads, crackers, cereals, grains, and starchy vegetables. One exchange of Bread is approximately 80 calories. Examples of one Bread choice or exchange:

> 1 slice bread or 2 slices reduced-calorie bread (40 calories or less)
> 1 roll, any type (1 ounce)
> ½ cup cooked pasta or ¾ ounce uncooked (scant ½ cup)
> ½ cup cooked rice or 1 ounce uncooked (⅓ cup)
> 3 tablespoons flour
> ¾ ounce cold cereal
> ½ cup cooked hot cereal or ¾ ounce uncooked (2 tablespoons)
> ½ cup corn (kernels or cream style) or peas
> 4 ounces white potato, cooked, or 5 ounces uncooked
> 3 ounces sweet potato, cooked, or 4 ounces uncooked
> 3 cups air-popped popcorn
> 7 fat-free crackers (¾ ounce)
> 3 (2½-inch squares) graham crackers
> 2 (¾-ounce) rice cakes or 6 mini
> 1 tortilla, any type (6-inch diameter)

Fruits

All fruits and fruit juices. One exchange of Fruit is approximately 60 calories. Examples of one Fruit choice or exchange:

1 small apple or ½ cup slices
1 small orange
½ medium banana
¾ cup berries (except strawberries and cranberries)
1 cup strawberries or cranberries
½ cup canned fruit, packed in fruit juice or rinsed well
2 tablespoons raisins
1 tablespoon spreadable fruit spread
½ cup apple juice (4 fluid ounces)
½ cup orange juice (4 fluid ounces)
½ cup applesauce

Fat-Free Milk

Milk, buttermilk, and yogurt. One exchange of Fat-Free Milk is approximately 90 calories. Examples of one Fat-Free Milk choice or exchange:

1 cup fat-free milk
½ cup evaporated fat-free milk
1 cup low-fat buttermilk
¾ cup plain fat-free yogurt
⅓ cup nonfat dry milk powder

Vegetables

All fresh, canned, or frozen vegetables other than the starchy vegetables. One exchange of Vegetable is approximately 30 calories. Examples of one Vegetable choice or exchange:

½ cup vegetable
¼ cup tomato sauce
1 medium fresh tomato
½ cup vegetable juice
1 cup shredded lettuce or cabbage

Fats

Margarine, mayonnaise, vegetable oils, salad dressings, olives, and nuts. One exchange of Fat is approximately 40 calories. Examples of one Fat choice or exchange:

1 teaspoon margarine or 2 teaspoons reduced-calorie margarine
1 teaspoon butter
1 teaspoon vegetable oil
1 teaspoon mayonnaise or 2 teaspoons reduced-calorie mayonnaise
1 teaspoon peanut butter
1 ounce olives
¼ ounce pecans or walnuts

Free Foods

Foods that do not provide nutritional value but are used to enhance the taste of foods are included in the Free Foods group. Examples of these are spices, herbs, extracts, vinegar, lemon juice, mustard, Worcestershire sauce, and soy sauce. Cooking sprays and artificial sweeteners used in moderation are also included in this group. However, you'll see that I include the caloric value of artificial sweeteners in the Optional Calories of the recipes.

You may occasionally see a recipe that lists "free food" as part of the portion. According to the published exchange lists, a free food contains fewer than 20 calories per serving. Two or three servings per day of free foods/drinks are usually allowed in a meal plan.

Optional Calories

Foods that do not fit into any other group but are used in moderation in recipes are included in Optional Calories. Foods that are counted in this way include sugar-free gelatin and puddings, fat-free mayonnaise and dressings, reduced-calorie whipped toppings, reduced-calorie syrups and jams, chocolate chips, coconut, and canned broth.

Sliders™

These are 80 Optional Calorie increments that do not fit into any particular category. You can choose which food group to *slide* these into. It is wise to limit this selection to approximately three to four per day to ensure the best possible nutrition for your body while still enjoying an occasional treat.

Sliders may be used in either of the following ways:

1. If you have consumed all your Protein, Bread, Fruit, or Fat-Free Milk Weight Loss Choices for the day, and you want to eat additional foods from those food groups, you simply use a Slider. It's what I call "healthy horse trading." Remember that Sliders may not be traded for choices in the Vegetables or Fats food groups.

2. Sliders may also be deducted from your Optional Calories for the day or week. One-quarter Slider equals 20 Optional Calories; ½ Slider equals 40 Optional Calories; ¾ Slider equals 60 Optional Calories; and 1 Slider equals 80 Optional Calories.

Healthy Exchanges

Weight Loss

Choices

My original Healthy Exchanges program of Weight Loss Choices was based on an average daily total of 1,400 to 1,600 calories per day. That was what I determined was right for my needs, and for those of most women. Because men require additional calories (about 1,600 to 1,900), here are my suggested plans for women and men. (*If you require more or fewer calories, please revise this plan to meet your individual needs.*)

Each day, women should plan to eat:

2 Fat-Free Milk choices, 90 calories each
2 Fat choices, 40 calories each
3 Fruit choices, 60 calories each
4 Vegetable choices or more, 30 calories each
5 Protein choices, 60 calories each
5 Bread choices, 80 calories each

Each day, men should plan to eat:

2 Fat-Free Milk choices, 90 calories each
4 Fat choices, 40 calories each
3 Fruit choices, 60 calories each
4 Vegetable choices or more, 30 calories each
6 Protein choices, 60 calories each
7 Bread choices, 80 calories each

Young people should follow the program for men but add 1 Fat-Free Milk choice for a total of 3 servings.

You may also choose to add up to 100 Optional Calories per day, and up to 21 to 28 Sliders per week at 80 calories each. If you choose to include more Sliders in your daily or weekly totals, deduct those 80 calories from your Optional Calorie "bank."

A word about **Sliders**: These are to be counted toward your totals after you have used your allotment of choices of Fat-Free Milk, Protein, Bread, and Fruit for the day. By "sliding" an additional choice into one of these groups, you can meet your individual needs for that day. Sliders are especially helpful when traveling, stressed-out, eating out, or for special events. I often use mine so I can enjoy my favorite Healthy Exchanges desserts. Vegetables are not to be counted as Sliders. Enjoy as many Vegetable choices as you need to feel satisfied. Because we want to limit our fat intake to moderate amounts, additional Fat choices should not be counted as Sliders. If you choose to include more fat on an *occasional* basis, count the extra choices as Optional Calories.

Keep a daily food diary of your Weight Loss Choices, checking off what you eat as you go. If, at the end of the day, your required selections are not 100 percent accounted for, but you have done the best you can, go to bed with a clear conscience. There will be days when you have ¼ Fruit or ½ Bread left over. What are you going to do—eat two slices of an orange or half a slice of bread and throw the rest out? I always say, "Nothing in life comes out exact." Just do the best you can . . . *the best you can.*

Try to drink at least eight 8-ounce glasses of water a day. Water truly is the "nectar" of good health.

As a little added insurance, I take a multivitamin each day. It's not essential, but if my day's worth of well-planned meals "bites the dust" when unexpected events intrude on my regular routine, my body still gets its vital nutrients.

The calories listed in each group of Choices are averages. Some choices within each group may be higher or lower, so it's important to select a variety of different foods instead of eating the same three or four all the time.

Use your Optional Calories! They are what I call "life's little extras." They make all the difference in how you enjoy your food and appreciate the variety available to you. Yes, we can get by without them, but do you really want to? Keep in mind that you should be using all your daily Weight Loss Choices first to ensure you are getting the basics of good nutrition. But I guarantee that Optional Calories will keep you from feeling deprived—and help you reach your weight-loss goals.

Spectacularly Smooth: Tips for Making Great Smoothies Every Time

Smoothie recipes are among the simplest you'll ever read—a list of ingredients usually all tossed into a blender compartment and quickly whipped, chopped, pureed, and liquefied into a rich, thick, practically perfect fruit shake. Here's the thing, though: getting the best possible results is more likely when you follow some simple rules and easy tips for making these nutritious and delicious drinks.

1. New smoothie machines and some blenders can break up ice cubes without any problem, so you may not need to worry about using only crushed ice in my smoothie recipes. According to my tests, about 12 large or 18 small ice cubes will produce 1 cup of crushed ice. But if you have an older or less powerful model, and if your refrigerator does not have a crushed ice option, here is **a very easy way to make crushed ice**: Fill your blender jar about halfway with cold water. Add about 2 cups of ice cubes.

Place the lid on the blender jar. Press and release the "chop" button three or four times or until the ice cubes are crushed to the desired consistency. Pour the entire contents into a colander to drain off the water. This process will make about 1 cup crushed ice.

2. **Fresh fruit**, picked and purchased at its ripest, makes truly delicious smoothies. This is a good reason to buy your fruit at farmstands or farmers' markets, if you have that option. But if your only choice is a supermarket, talk to the fruit manager about when he or she gets deliveries, so you get "first pick." And if you've got a choice among supermarkets in your town, visit all of them to decide which one offers you the best possible fruit choice.

3. If your fruit isn't fully ripe when you bring it home, try placing it inside a paper or plastic bag to ripen. Some fruit ripens quickly by this method, so keep checking on it. Fruit tends to have the best flavor when stored in a bowl on the table or counter, not in the refrigerator. **How can you tell if fruit is ripe?** Everyone has a different system, but for me, fruit is best when its scent is sweet and its flesh bounces slightly back when pressed with a fingertip. Someone once taught me that a pineapple is ripe when you can pull one of its leaves free without any effort.

4. Frozen fruit is a great ingredient for easy smoothies. You don't have to shop for different fruits (if you buy a frozen mélange), and you don't have to cut it up. It's ready anytime you open the freezer (as long as you remembered to pick it up at the store)! Frozen fruit is often better tasting than some fresh. Why? Because it's flash-frozen minutes after it's picked, while some fresh fruit languishes in store bins or travels many miles from farm to market before it reaches you. Make sure you purchase **unsweetened frozen fruit**, not fruit that has had syrup added to it. You can **freeze your own** fresh fruit for use in your smoothies, too. If you're lucky enough to have an orchard or even just one great peach tree, peel, dice, and freeze your fruit in sturdy bags. Label it by date so you use the oldest fruit first.

5. You'll notice that I use lots of **canned fruit** in my smoothie recipes, though other smoothie books may "turn up their noses" at this handy, healthy convenience food. I also use plenty of fresh and frozen fruits—but I believe in giving my readers as many options as possible. For those of us who live in areas where the choices of fresh and frozen fruit are often limited, canned fruit provides wonderful variety when it comes to making smoothies. Another reason for feeling good about using canned fruit is this: it blends beautifully, and in addition to providing great taste, it acts as part "liquid" and part "thickener" once it's blended with other ingredients.

6. Once you start making smoothies, I suspect you'll be preparing them often, so why not streamline the process by **buying a week or so's worth of fruit at a time**? Turn on your kitchen radio or TV, then peel, chop, and bag it all. You'll be grateful for the timesaving help later in the week.

7. **Drink your smoothies immediately**, or as soon as possible after you stop the blender and pour them out. Within minutes, fruit can begin to turn brown, and drinks with yogurt in them often start to separate.

8. **Buy the best blender you can afford**. I tested every one of these recipes on a very basic blender, but I also tried them on stronger models with more speeds and options. If you're going to be making smoothies for a large family, consider investing in a sturdy, newer model. Ask friends for recommendations or check out *Consumer Reports*. Remember: More speeds doesn't always mean a better result. The size and strength of the motor is probably the most important feature in a blender.

9. When my recipes call for fresh fruit, you can also use fresh fruit that has been frozen, even partially. In most cases, **the colder your fruit, the thicker your finished smoothie**.

10. **Always start with liquids** when you are making a smoothie. Then, add your solids on top. As the liquids begins to "hold hands" with your fruit chunks, the shake begins to form properly.

11. **Start your blender on a low speed** at first, so that it can chop the fruit into ever smaller pieces. Finish on high, pureeing the contents and whipping it up into a delectable froth.
12. **Never stir the contents of your blender while the blade is moving and the motor is running**. It's dangerous! Turn it off first, then stir from the bottom up to combine liquids and solids for better results.

Now, you're the only one who can decide how thick and how sweet you like your smoothies. When I tested these recipes, I went for "middle-of-the-road" in both categories. If you think your smoothie is **too thick**, and you want to add more liquid, I advise using water or Diet Mountain Dew so you don't change the nutritional values of the recipe. (Or you could serve it with a spoon like a frozen dessert.) If it's **too thin**, add a little ice and keep blending.

I've aimed for a level of sweetness that will please most people, but if you like things sweet, add more Splenda a little at a time and keep tasting. If you like foods less sweet, adjust the recipe up front and see if you need less than I advise.

There, you're ready to go. Ladies and gentlemen, start your blenders!

JoAnna's Ten Commandments of Successful Cooking

A very important part of any journey is knowing where you are going and the best way to get there. If you plan and prepare before you start to cook, you should reach mealtime with foods to write home about!

1. **Read the entire recipe from start to finish** and be sure you understand the process involved. Check that you have all the equipment you will need *before* you begin.
2. **Check the ingredient list** and be sure you have *everything* and in the amounts required. Keep cooking sprays handy—while they're not listed as ingredients, I use them all the time (just a quick squirt!).
3. **Set out *all* the ingredients and equipment needed** to prepare the recipe on the counter near you *before* you start. Remember that old saying *A stitch in time saves nine?* It applies in the kitchen, too.
4. **Do as much advance preparation as possible** before actually cooking. Chop, cut, grate, or do whatever is needed to prepare the ingredients and have them ready before you start to mix. Turn the oven on at least ten min-

utes before putting food in to bake, to allow the oven to preheat to the proper temperature.

5. **Use a kitchen timer** to tell you when the cooking or baking time is up. Because stove temperatures vary slightly by manufacturer, you may want to set your timer for five minutes less than the suggested time just to prevent overcooking. Check the progress of your dish at that time, then decide if you need the additional minutes or not.

6. **Measure carefully.** Use glass measures for liquids and metal or plastic cups for dry ingredients. My recipes are based on standard measurements. Unless I tell you it's a scant or full cup, measure the cup level.

7. **For best results, follow the recipe instructions exactly.** Feel free to substitute ingredients that *don't tamper* with the basic chemistry of the recipe, but be sure to leave key ingredients alone. For example, you could substitute sugar-free instant chocolate pudding for sugar-free instant butterscotch pudding, but if you used a six-serving package when a four-serving package was listed in the ingredients, or you used instant when cook-and-serve is required, you won't get the right result.

8. **Clean up as you go.** It is much easier to wash a few items at a time than to face a whole counter of dirty dishes later. The same is true for spills on the counter or floor.

9. **Be careful about doubling or halving a recipe.** Though many recipes can be altered successfully to serve more or fewer people, *many cannot.* This is especially true when it comes to spices and liquids. If you try to double a recipe that calls for 1 teaspoon pumpkin-pie spice, for example, and you double the spice, you may end up with a too-spicy taste. I usually suggest increasing spices or liquid by 1½ times when doubling a recipe. If it tastes a little bland to you, you can increase the spice to 1¾ times the original amount the next time you prepare the dish. Remember: You can always add more, but you can't take it out after it's stirred in.

The same is true with liquid ingredients. If you wanted to **triple** a main dish recipe because you were planning to serve a crowd, you might think you should use three times as much of every ingredient. Don't, or you could end up with soup instead! If the original recipe calls for 1¾ cup tomato sauce, I'd suggest using 3½ cups when you **triple** the recipe (or 2¾ cups if you **double** it). You'll still have a good-tasting dish that won't run all over the plate.

10. **Write your reactions next to each recipe once you've served it.** Yes, that's right, I'm giving you permission to write in this book. It's yours, after all. Ask yourself: Did everyone like it? Did you have to add another half teaspoon of chili seasoning to please your family, who like to live on the spicier side of the street? You may even want to rate the recipe on a scale of 1 ☆ to 4 ☆, depending on what you thought of it. (Four stars would be the top rating—and I hope you'll feel that way about many of my recipes.) Jotting down your comments while they are fresh in your mind will help you personalize the recipe to your own taste the next time you prepare it.

The Recipes

How to Read a Healthy Exchanges Recipe

The Healthy Exchanges Nutritional Analysis

Before using these recipes, you may wish to consult your physician or health-care provider to be sure they are appropriate for you. The information in this book is not intended to take the place of any medical advice. It reflects my experiences, studies, research, and opinions regarding healthy eating.

Each recipe includes nutritional information calculated in three ways:

> *Healthy Exchanges Weight Loss Choices™ or Exchanges*
> *Calories; Fat, Protein, Carbohydrates, and Fiber in grams; Sodium*
> *and Calcium in milligrams*
> *Diabetic Exchanges*

In every Healthy Exchanges recipe, the Diabetic Exchanges have been calculated by a registered dietitian. All the other calculations were done by computer, using the Food Processor II software. When the ingredient listing gives more than one choice, the first ingredient listed is the one used in the recipe analysis. Due to inevitable variations in the ingredients you choose to use, the nutritional values should be considered approximate.

The annotation "(limited)" following Protein counts in some recipes indicates that consumption of whole eggs should be limited to four per week.

Please note the following symbols:

☆ *This star means read the recipe's directions carefully for special instructions about* **division** *of ingredients.*

❋ *This symbol indicates* **FREEZES WELL.**

Dairy-Free Delights

If you've always believed that a smoothie just isn't a smoothie without some milk or yogurt, I'm happy to tell you otherwise! Super-duper fruit shakes made from just about every kind of fresh, frozen, or canned fruit, are a splendid way to get your "daily five" and add so much nutrition and energy to your daily diet.

I've suggested some fun combinations, from cranberries coupled with pears to kiwifruit partnered with peaches, but really, anything is possible! Choose what you like, make use of what's in the refrigerator and freezer, and blend away!

Dairy-Free Delights

Fresh Rhubarb Smoothie

What a pleasing way to enjoy these crunchy fruit stalks, combined with the sweet sensation of pineapple! You'll feel good health in every part of your body as you drink this flavorful fruit shake.

◑ Serves 2 (1 cup)

> 1 (8-ounce) can crushed pineapple, packed in fruit juice,
>> undrained
> 1 cup diced fresh rhubarb
> ½ cup Splenda Granular
> 1 cup crushed ice

In a blender container, combine undrained pineapple, rhubarb, Splenda, and ice. Cover and process on BLEND for 50 to 60 seconds or until mixture is smooth. Evenly pour into 2 glasses. Serve at once.

Each serving equals:

HE: 1 Fruit • 1 Vegetable • ¼ Slider • 4 Optional Calories

76 Calories • 0 gm Fat • 1 gm Protein • 18 gm Carbohydrate • 3 mg Sodium • 69 mg Calcium • 2 gm Fiber

DIABETIC EXCHANGES: 1 Fruit

Mango and Pineapple Smoothie

You will taste the exotic glory of the tropics in each sip of this fresh-and-fruity concoction. Make sure you choose the ripest mangos you can find!   ☻   Serves 2 (1½ cups)

> ½ cup cold Diet Mountain Dew
> 2 tablespoons Splenda Granular
> 1 (8-ounce) can crushed pineapple, packed in fruit juice,
>   undrained
> 1 cup (2 medium) peeled and sliced fresh ripe mango
> 1 cup crushed ice

In a blender container, combine Diet Mountain Dew, Splenda, undrained pineapple, and mango. Cover and process on BLEND for 20 seconds. Add ice. Re-cover and process on BLEND for 25 to 30 seconds or until mixture is smooth. Evenly pour into 2 glasses. Serve at once.

HINT: 1 cup sliced canned mango, drained, may be used in place
    of fresh mango.

Each serving equals:

HE: 2 Fruit • 6 Optional Calories

96 Calories • 0 gm Fat • 1 gm Protein •
23 gm Carbohydrate • 11 mg Sodium •
25 mg Calcium • 2 gm Fiber

DIABETIC EXCHANGES: 2 Fruit

Mango Smoothie

There was a time when fresh mango was never seen in our Midwestern supermarkets, but times have changed, and deliciously so. Now the sky's the limit when it comes to choosing great fresh fruit to enjoy every day! ☺ Serves 2 (1¼ cups)

1 cup (2 medium) peeled and sliced fresh ripe mango
½ cup cold unsweetened orange juice
1 cup crushed ice

In a blender container, combine mango, orange juice, and ice. Cover and process on BLEND for 20 to 25 seconds or until mixture is smooth. Evenly pour into 2 glasses. Serve at once.

HINT: 1 cup sliced canned mango, drained, may be used in place of fresh mango.

Each serving equals:

HE: 1½ Fruit

---

84 Calories • 0 gm Fat • 1 gm Protein •
20 gm Carbohydrate • 3 mg Sodium •
13 mg Calcium • 1 gm Fiber

DIABETIC EXCHANGES: 1½ Fruit

Mango Tango Smoothie

Just as no one can resist the beat of a smooth and slinky tango number, no one can resist the siren call of this tempting taste treat rich in vitamin C! Don't be surprised by my use of Diet Mountain Dew—it has a terrific citrusy flavor.   ☻   Serves 2

½ cup (1 medium) peeled and sliced fresh ripe mango
½ cup cold unsweetened orange juice
2 tablespoons Splenda Granular
¾ cup cold Diet Mountain Dew
1 cup crushed ice

In a blender container, combine mango, orange juice, Splenda, and Diet Mountain Dew. Cover and process on BLEND for 15 seconds. Add ice. Re-cover and process on BLEND for 25 to 30 seconds or until mixture is smooth. Evenly pour into 2 glasses. Serve at once.

HINT: ½ cup sliced canned mango, drained, may be used in place of fresh mango.

Each serving equals:

HE: 1 Fruit

52 Calories • 0 gm Fat • 0 gm Protein •
13 gm Carbohydrate • 11 mg Sodium •
9 mg Calcium • 1 gm Fiber

DIABETIC EXCHANGES: 1 Fruit

Starburst Smoothie

This time, the fireworks will explode delectably inside your mouth, as you revel in a wonderful combo of fun fruits! This is so special, you could serve it at a festive cocktail party.

☉ Serves 2 (1¼ cups)

> *1 kiwifruit, peeled and diced*
> *1 cup (1 medium) sliced banana*
> *¼ cup cold Diet Mountain Dew*
> *1 cup frozen unsweetened strawberries*
> *1 cup crushed ice*

In a blender container, combine kiwi, banana, and Diet Mountain Dew. Cover and process on BLEND for 15 seconds. Add strawberries. Re-cover and process on BLEND for 20 seconds. Add ice. Re-cover and process on BLEND for 15 to 20 seconds or until mixture is smooth. Evenly pour into 2 glasses. Serve at once.

Each serving equals:

HE: 2 Fruit

---

136 Calories • 0 gm Fat • 2 gm Protein •
32 gm Carbohydrate • 6 mg Sodium •
37 mg Calcium • 5 gm Fiber

DIABETIC EXCHANGES: 2 Fruit

Kiwi Peach Smoothie

One of the challenges of creating recipes for irresistible smoothies is figuring out which ingredients to send on a culinary "blind date" and see what develops! This time, I've entangled sweet peaches with kiwis, those fascinating fruits all the way from New Zealand. It's a fine romance! ☻ Serves 2 (1 cup)

1 (8-ounce) can sliced peaches, packed in fruit juice, undrained
2 kiwifruit, peeled and diced
2 tablespoons Splenda Granular
1 cup crushed ice

In a blender container, combine undrained peaches, kiwi, and Splenda. Cover and process on BLEND for 20 seconds. Add ice. Re-cover and process on BLEND for 15 to 20 seconds or until mixture is smooth. Evenly pour into 2 glasses. Serve at once.

Each serving equals:

HE: 2 Fruit

116 Calories • 0 gm Fat • 1 gm Protein •
28 gm Carbohydrate • 18 mg Sodium •
30 mg Calcium • 3 gm Fiber

DIABETIC EXCHANGES: 2 Fruit

Frosted Strawberry Smoothie

There are so many luscious shades of pink, every one of them plea-surable, and every one reminds me of my favorite heavenly fruit, the strawberry. Here's a charming way to celebrate its glories in icy splendor, one that I know will appeal to my son Tommy!

◑ Serves 2 (1½ cups)

> 1 cup cold unsweetened orange juice
> ½ cup cold Diet Mountain Dew
> ¼ cup Splenda Granular
> 2 cups frozen unsweetened strawberries
> ½ cup crushed ice

In a blender container, combine orange juice, Diet Mountain Dew, and Splenda. Cover and process on BLEND for 10 seconds. Add strawberries. Re-cover and process on BLEND for 30 seconds. Add ice. Re-cover and process on BLEND for 15 to 20 seconds or until mixture is smooth. Evenly pour into 2 glasses. Serve at once.

Each serving equals:

HE: 2 Fruit • 12 Optional Calories

136 Calories • 0 gm Fat • 1 gm Protein •
33 gm Carbohydrate • 13 mg Sodium •
45 mg Calcium • 5 gm Fiber

DIABETIC EXCHANGES: 2 Fruit

Strawberry Daiquiri Smoothie

So many people have chosen to omit alcohol from their diet for health or other personal reasons, but that's no reason not to enjoy party drinks served alcohol-free. This is a festive beverage of intense flavor, so invite your guests to partake and party on!

◐ Serves 2 (1½ cups)

> 1 cup cold Diet Mountain Dew
> ¼ cup Splenda Granular
> 1 tablespoon lime juice
> 1 tablespoon lemon juice
> 1 teaspoon rum extract
> 2 cups frozen unsweetened strawberries, coarsely chopped
> 3 to 4 drops red food coloring, optional

In a blender container, combine Diet Mountain Dew, Splenda, lime juice, lemon juice, and rum extract. Cover and process on BLEND for 10 seconds. Add strawberries and red food coloring, if desired. Re-cover and process on BLEND for 30 to 45 seconds or until mixture is smooth. Evenly pour into 2 glasses. Serve at once.

Each serving equals:

HE: 1 Fruit • 12 Optional Calories

92 Calories • 0 gm Fat • 1 gm Protein •
22 gm Carbohydrate • 16 mg Sodium •
36 mg Calcium • 4 gm Fiber

DIABETIC EXCHANGES: 1 Fruit

Cliff's Special Smoothie

Isn't it wonderful that we can take something tart and terrific, then sweeten it up? For anyone who thinks grapefruit juice is too sour, give your taste buds a chance to try it in this special combination. Cliff is its greatest cheerleader!   ◐   Serves 2 (1 cup)

> 1 (6-ounce) can grapefruit juice
> 1/4 cup cold Diet Mountain Dew
> 1/4 cup Splenda Granular
> 1 cup frozen unsweetened strawberries

In a blender container, combine grapefruit juice, Diet Mountain Dew, and Splenda. Cover and process on BLEND for 10 seconds. Add strawberries. Re-cover and process on BLEND for 30 to 35 seconds or until mixture is smooth. Evenly pour into 2 glasses. Serve at once.

Each serving equals:

HE: 1¼ Fruit • 6 Optional Calories

88 Calories • 0 gm Fat • 1 gm Protein • 21 gm Carbohydrate • 6 mg Sodium • 25 mg Calcium • 2 gm Fiber

DIABETIC EXCHANGES: 1 Fruit

Pears Perfect Smoothie

I've always believed in using the best canned and frozen products in my recipes, and here's a wonderful example of how to do it well. Even if you haven't got a piece of ripe fruit in the house, you can still enjoy a healthy smoothie anytime!   ☻   Serves 2 (1 cup)

> 1 (8-ounce) can pear halves, packed in fruit juice, undrained
> ½ cup cold Diet Mountain Dew
> 1 cup frozen unsweetened strawberries

In a blender container, combine undrained pears and Diet Mountain Dew. Cover and process on BLEND for 15 seconds. Add strawberries. Re-cover and process on BLEND for 15 to 20 seconds or until mixture is smooth. Evenly pour into 2 glasses. Serve at once.

Each serving equals:

HE: 1½ Fruit

---

112 Calories • 0 gm Fat • 0 gm Protein •
28 gm Carbohydrate • 17 mg Sodium •
18 mg Calcium • 4 gm Fiber

DIABETIC EXCHANGES: 1½ Fruit

Cranberry Pear Smoothie

You may decide to keep your canned fruit in the refrigerator, to make your smoothies even cooler. This blend of juicy canned pears with cranberry juice is oh-so-easy and oh-so-good!

● Serves 2 (1¼ cups)

> 1 (8-ounce) can pear halves, packed in fruit juice, undrained
> 1 cup cold Ocean Spray cranberry juice cocktail
> 2 tablespoons Splenda Granular
> 1 cup crushed ice

In a blender container, combine undrained pears, cranberry juice cocktail, and Splenda. Cover and process on BLEND for 20 seconds. Add ice. Re-cover and process on BLEND for 25 to 30 seconds or until mixture is smooth. Evenly pour into 2 glasses. Serve at once.

Each serving equals:

HE: 1½ Fruit • 6 Optional Calories

104 Calories • 0 gm Fat • 0 gm Protein •
26 gm Carbohydrate • 12 mg Sodium •
11 mg Calcium • 2 gm Fiber

DIABETIC EXCHANGES: 1½ Fruit

Sweet Dreams Smoothie

I didn't create this recipe to honor the great singer Patsy Cline, who sang "Sweet Dreams" so unforgettably, but now that I've tasted it, I think it does the lady justice! It's a great choice for an evening snack before a good night's rest.   ☻   Serves 2 (1 cup)

> 1 (8-ounce) can pear halves, packed in fruit juice, undrained
> 1 (8-ounce) can crushed pineapple, packed in fruit juice,
>   undrained
> 1/4 teaspoon almond extract
> 1/2 cup crushed ice

In a blender container, combine undrained pears, undrained pineapple, and almond extract. Cover and process on BLEND for 20 seconds. Add ice. Re-cover and process on BLEND for 30 to 35 seconds or until mixture is smooth. Evenly pour into 2 glasses. Serve at once.

Each serving equals:

HE: 2 Fruit

112 Calories • 0 gm Fat • 0 gm Protein •
28 gm Carbohydrate • 10 mg Sodium •
17 mg Calcium • 3 gm Fiber

DIABETIC EXCHANGES: 2 Fruit

P & P Smoothie

P is for pleasure, and P is for pizzazz, and this P & P recipe has plenty of both! If your plan is to eat well and feel great, put this smoothie on the menu!　　❂　　Serves 2 (1½ cups)

> 1 (8-ounce) can sliced peaches, packed in fruit juice, undrained
> 1 (8-ounce) can crushed pineapple, packed in fruit juice,
>   undrained
> ½ cup cold Diet Mountain Dew
> 2 tablespoons Splenda Granular
> 1½ cups crushed ice

In a blender container, combine undrained peaches, undrained pineapple, Diet Mountain Dew, and Splenda. Cover and process on BLEND for 15 seconds. Add ice. Re-cover and process on BLEND for 15 to 20 seconds or until mixture is smooth. Evenly pour into 2 glasses. Serve at once.

Each serving equals:

HE: 2 Fruit • 6 Optional Calories

112 Calories • 0 gm Fat • 0 gm Protein •
28 gm Carbohydrate • 24 mg Sodium •
16 mg Calcium • 2 gm Fiber

DIABETIC EXCHANGES: 1½ Fruit

Blue Ribbon Smoothie

The key to delicious smoothie recipes is figuring out just the right amount of sweetness needed in each one. Here, you get a great jolt of natural sweetness in both the peaches and cherries, so I only needed to add a bit of sweetener to make it a prizewinner!

○ Serves 2 (1 full cup)

> 1 (8-ounce) can sliced peaches, packed in fruit juice, undrained
> ½ cup cold unsweetened orange juice
> 2 tablespoons Splenda Granular
> ½ cup frozen unsweetened bing or dark sweet cherries
> 1 cup crushed ice

In a blender container, combine undrained peaches, orange juice, and Splenda. Cover and process on BLEND for 15 seconds. Add cherries and ice. Re-cover and process on BLEND for 30 to 35 seconds or until mixture is smooth. Evenly pour into 2 glasses. Serve at once.

Each serving equals:

HE: 2 Fruit • 3 Optional Calories

---

124 Calories • 0 gm Fat • 1 gm Protein •
30 gm Carbohydrate • 19 mg Sodium •
10 mg Calcium • 2 gm Fiber

DIABETIC EXCHANGES: 2 Fruit

Banana Split Smoothie

What fun—to enjoy a smoothie that joins all the fantastic flavors of the richest dessert in town! Bananas are a terrific way to sweeten and thicken any smoothie, you'll discover.

◐ Serves 4 (1 cup)

> 1 cup (1 medium) diced banana
> 1 (8-ounce) can crushed pineapple, packed in fruit juice, undrained
> 1 cup cold Diet Mountain Dew
> 2 tablespoons Splenda Granular
> 2 cups frozen unsweetened strawberries ☆
> ¼ cup Cool Whip Lite
> 2 maraschino cherries, halved

In a blender container, combine banana, undrained pineapple, Diet Mountain Dew, and Splenda. Cover and process on BLEND for 15 seconds. Add 1 cup strawberries. Recover and process on BLEND for 20 seconds. Add remaining 1 cup strawberries. Recover and process on BLEND for 25 to 30 seconds or until mixture is smooth. Evenly pour into 4 glasses. Top each with 1 tablespoon Cool Whip Lite and ½ maraschino cherry half. Serve at once.

Each serving equals:

HE: 1½ Fruit • 18 Optional Calories

108 Calories • 0 gm Fat • 1 gm Protein • 26 gm Carbohydrate • 3 mg Sodium • 28 mg Calcium • 3 gm Fiber

DIABETIC EXCHANGES: 1½ Fruit

Banana Sunshine Smoothie

When the weather outside is gray and cloudy, when the thermometer hovers around zero, you need warmth and sunshine any way you can get it—and here's one of my new favorites!

◐ Serves 2 (1 cup)

½ cup cold unsweetened orange juice

1 cup (1 medium) diced banana

2 tablespoons Splenda Granular

1 cup crushed ice

In a blender container, combine orange juice, banana, and Splenda. Cover and process on BLEND for 10 seconds. Add ice. Recover and process on BLEND for 25 to 30 seconds or until mixture is smooth. Evenly pour into 2 glasses. Serve at once.

Each serving equals:

HE: 1½ Fruit • 6 Optional Calories

104 Calories • 0 gm Fat • 1 gm Protein • 25 gm Carbohydrate • 2 mg Sodium • 9 mg Calcium • 2 gm Fiber

DIABETIC EXCHANGES: 1½ Fruit

Tropical Smoothie

Can you taste and feel the sweet heat of a steamy vacation resort when you're drinking a cool and creamy smoothie? This flavor blend will convince you that you might even need a bit of sunblock to keep from sizzling!　　◐　　Serves 4 (1 cup)

> 1 (8-ounce) can crushed pineapple, packed in fruit juice,
>   undrained
> 1¼ cups cold Diet Mountain Dew
> 2 cups frozen unsweetened strawberries, coarsely chopped
> 1 cup (1 medium) sliced banana
> 1 teaspoon coconut extract
> 1 cup crushed ice
> ¼ cup Cool Whip Lite
> 2 teaspoons flaked coconut

In a blender container, combine undrained pineapple and Diet Mountain Dew. Cover and process on BLEND for 20 seconds. Add strawberries, banana, coconut extract, and ice. Re-cover and process on BLEND for 25 to 30 seconds or until mixture is smooth. Evenly pour into 4 glasses. When serving, top each glass with 1 tablespoon Cool Whip Lite and ½ teaspoon coconut.

Each serving equals:

HE: 1½ Fruit • 17 Optional Calories

100 Calories • 0 gm Fat • 1 gm Protein •
24 gm Carbohydrate • 6 mg Sodium •
28 mg Calcium • 4 gm Fiber

DIABETIC EXCHANGES: 1½ Fruit

Catalina Sunrise Smoothie

The colors of a beautiful dawn seem to promise a wonderful day ahead, don't they? And when that sun rises over an island in the greatest ocean of all, what a day it's going to be!

⊙ Serves 2 (1¼ cups)

> 1 cup (1 medium) diced banana
> ½ cup cold unsweetened orange juice
> ½ cup cold Diet Mountain Dew
> 2 tablespoons Splenda Granular
> 1 cup frozen unsweetened strawberries

In a blender container, combine banana, orange juice, Diet Mountain Dew, and Splenda. Cover and process on BLEND for 15 seconds. Add strawberries. Re-cover and process on BLEND for 20 to 25 seconds or until mixture is smooth. Evenly pour into 2 glasses. Serve at once.

Each serving equals:

HE: 2 Fruit • 6 Optional Calories

136 Calories • 0 gm Fat • 1 gm Protein •
33 gm Carbohydrate • 10 mg Sodium •
27 mg Calcium • 4 gm Fiber

DIABETIC EXCHANGES: 2 Fruit

Trade Winds Smoothie

If you've never heard of the trade winds, they're the enticing breezes that persuaded sailors to travel for weeks and months in search of new lands and new flavors. I hope this swirl of sensational fruits and juice sends you on a joyful journey today!

○ Serves 4 (1½ cups)

> 1 cup (1 medium) diced banana
> 1 (8-ounce) can apricots, packed in fruit juice, undrained
> 1 (8-ounce) can crushed pineapple, packed in fruit juice, undrained
> 2 tablespoons Splenda Granular
> 1 teaspoon lime juice
> 1½ cups crushed ice

In a blender container, combine banana, undrained apricots, undrained pineapple, Splenda, and lime juice. Cover and process on BLEND for 20 seconds. Add ice. Re-cover and process on BLEND for 15 to 20 seconds or until mixture is smooth. Evenly pour into 4 glasses. Serve at once.

Each serving equals:

HE: 1½ Fruit • 3 Optional Calories

---

84 Calories • 0 gm Fat • 1 gm Protein •
20 gm Carbohydrate • 3 mg Sodium •
17 mg Calcium • 2 gm Fiber

DIABETIC EXCHANGES: 1½ Fruit

Tri-Fruit Smoothie

If one is good and two is better, then three spirited fruits in one delectable drink has got to be the best of all possible places to be! As they used to say in the 1920s, this one is definitely "the berries"!

◐ Serves 2 (1 full cup)

> 1 cup (1 medium) sliced banana
> 1¼ cups cold Diet Mountain Dew
> 2 tablespoons Splenda Granular
> 1 cup frozen unsweetened strawberries
> ¾ cup frozen unsweetened blueberries

In a blender container, combine banana, Diet Mountain Dew, and Splenda. Cover and process on BLEND for 15 seconds. Add strawberries and blueberries. Re-cover and process on BLEND for 30 to 35 seconds or until mixture is smooth. Evenly pour into 2 glasses. Serve at once.

Each serving equals:

HE: 2 Fruit • 6 Optional Calories

144 Calories • 0 gm Fat • 1 gm Protein • 35 gm Carbohydrate • 12 mg Sodium • 27 mg Calcium • 5 gm Fiber

DIABETIC EXCHANGES: 2 Fruit

Blue Swirl Smoothie

Smoothie fans have told me they think blueberries are the sweetest frozen fruit of all, and that may be true. Add some rich banana chunks, and you've got an undeniably appealing treat that's a gorgeous color, too! ☻ Serves 2 (1 full cup)

> 1 cup (1 medium) diced banana
> ¾ cup cold Diet Mountain Dew
> 2 tablespoons Splenda Granular
> 1½ cups frozen unsweetened blueberries

In a blender container, combine banana, Diet Mountain Dew, and Splenda. Cover and process on BLEND for 15 seconds. Add blueberries. Re-cover and process on BLEND for 15 to 20 seconds or until mixture is smooth. Evenly pour into 2 glasses. Serve at once.

Each serving equals:

HE: 2 Fruit • 6 Optional Calories

132 Calories • 0 gm Fat • 1 gm Protein •
32 gm Carbohydrate • 8 mg Sodium •
14 mg Calcium • 5 gm Fiber

DIABETIC EXCHANGES: 2 Fruit

Mandarin Blush Smoothie

I've adored mandarin oranges since I was a child, and I've met so many people who remember their sweet joys as vividly as I do. Here's my version of mandarin "memories" for all of them—and for you, too!   ○   Serves 2 (1¼ cups)

> 1 (11-ounce) can mandarin oranges, rinsed and drained
> 1 (8-ounce) can crushed pineapple, packed in fruit juice,
>   undrained
> ⅓ cup cold Diet Mountain Dew
> 1 cup crushed ice

In a blender container, combine oranges, undrained pineapple, and Diet Mountain Dew. Cover and process on BLEND for 30 seconds. Add ice. Re-cover and process on BLEND for 30 to 35 seconds or until mixture is smooth. Evenly pour into 2 glasses. Serve at once.

Each serving equals:

HE: 2 Fruit

---

104 Calories • 0 gm Fat • 0 gm Protein •
26 gm Carbohydrate • 14 mg Sodium •
17 mg Calcium • 1 gm Fiber

DIABETIC EXCHANGES: 2 Fruit

Hawaiian Pineapple Smoothie

It's a dream destination for so many people, and for many, one that may never be visited for real. But you can experience the intense and enticing pleasure of that delightful place with every gulp of this glorious drink! ☻ Serves 2 (1½ cups)

> 2 (8-ounce) cans crushed pineapple, packed in fruit juice,
>   undrained
> ½ cup cold Diet Mountain Dew
> ¼ cup Splenda Granular
> 1 cup crushed ice

In a blender container, combine undrained pineapple, Diet Mountain Dew, and Splenda. Cover and process on BLEND for 15 seconds. Add ice. Re-cover and process on BLEND for 15 to 20 seconds or until mixture is smooth. Evenly pour into 2 glasses. Serve at once.

Each serving equals:

HE: 2 Fruit • 12 Optional Calories

---

100 Calories • 0 gm Fat • 1 gm Protein •
24 gm Carbohydrate • 14 mg Sodium •
38 mg Calcium • 2 gm Fiber

DIABETIC EXCHANGES: 2 Fruit

Pineapple Pleasure Smoothie

It's almost indescribable, the blend of luscious, velvety flavors in this smoother-than-smooth recipe! Elvis Presley was renowned for loving peanut-butter-and-banana sandwiches, and of course he made that marvelous movie *Blue Hawaii*. This one's for the King!

◐ Serves 2 (1 cup)

> 1 cup (1 medium) diced banana
> 2 tablespoons Peter Pan reduced-fat peanut butter
> 1 (8-ounce) can crushed pineapple, packed in fruit juice,
>   undrained
> ½ cup crushed ice

In a blender container, combine banana, peanut butter, and undrained pineapple. Cover and process on BLEND for 25 seconds. Add ice. Re-cover and process on BLEND for 15 to 20 seconds or until mixture is smooth. Evenly pour into 2 glasses. Serve at once.

Each serving equals:

HE: 2 Fruit • 1 Protein • 1 Fat

---

193 Calories • 5 gm Fat • 5 gm Protein •
32 gm Carbohydrate • 77 mg Sodium •
21 mg Calcium • 4 gm Fiber

DIABETIC EXCHANGES: 2 Fruit • ½ Meat • ½ Fat

Hawaiian Punch Smoothie

When I was testing recipes for this book, I enjoyed people's puzzled looks as they tried to figure out the ingredients in each tempting glass. When someone said this one tasted like a more spectacular Hawaiian Punch, I just smiled—and wrote it down!

◑   Serves 4 (1 cup)

> 1 (8-ounce) can crushed pineapple, packed in fruit juice,
>   undrained
> 1 cup cold unsweetened orange juice
> ½ cup cold Diet Mountain Dew
> 1 cup (1 medium) sliced banana
> 2 cups crushed ice

In a blender container, combine undrained pineapple, orange juice, and Diet Mountain Dew. Cover and process on BLEND for 15 seconds. Add banana and ice. Re-cover and process on BLEND for 20 to 30 seconds or until mixture is smooth. Evenly pour into 4 glasses. Serve at once.

Each serving equals:

HE: 1½ Fruit

80 Calories • 0 gm Fat • 1 gm Protein •
19 gm Carbohydrate • 2 mg Sodium •
16 mg Calcium • 1 gm Fiber

DIABETIC EXCHANGES: 1 Fruit

Crushed Melon Smoothie

For me, fresh melon is one of the real joys of summer, but these days we get beautiful melons year-round, even here in Iowa. By blending two of my favorites, I discovered that together they're even more spectacular than when enjoyed on their own!

◐ Serves 2 (1¼ cups)

1 cup diced cantaloupe
1 cup diced and seeded watermelon
¼ cup cold Diet Mountain Dew
1 cup crushed ice

In a blender container, combine cantaloupe, watermelon, Diet Mountain Dew, and ice. Cover and process on BLEND for 15 to 20 seconds or until mixture is smooth. Evenly pour into 2 glasses. Serve at once.

Each serving equals:

HE: 1 Fruit

56 Calories • 0 gm Fat • 1 gm Protein • 13 gm Carbohydrate • 12 mg Sodium • 14 mg Calcium • 1 gm Fiber

DIABETIC EXCHANGES: 1 Fruit

Cantaloupe Cooler Smoothie

Like all those yellow and orange vegetables, cantaloupe delivers lots of healthy vitamin A, but it's the flavor and the luscious color of this combination that made my mouth water! Let the sunshine in!

○ Serves 2 (1 cup)

1½ cups diced cantaloupe
½ cup cold unsweetened orange juice
2 tablespoons cold Diet Mountain Dew
2 tablespoons Splenda Granular
½ cup crushed ice

In a blender container, combine cantaloupe, orange juice, Diet Mountain Dew, and Splenda. Cover and process on BLEND for 20 seconds. Add ice. Re-cover and process on BLEND for 20 to 25 seconds. Evenly pour into 2 glasses. Serve at once.

Each serving equals:

HE: 1½ Fruit • 6 Optional Calories

72 Calories • 0 gm Fat • 1 gm Protein •
17 gm Carbohydrate • 13 mg Sodium •
18 mg Calcium • 1 gm Fiber

DIABETIC EXCHANGES: 1 Fruit

Fresh Plum Smoothie

It's important to peel your plums carefully for this recipe—no little bits of skin should compete with its velvety smoothness! I was fascinated to find what a great addition the nutmeg was, and I bet you will, too.　　◑　　Serves 4 (1 cup)

> 1 cup (4 medium) peeled, pitted, and halved fresh plums
> 1 cup cold Diet Mountain Dew
> 1/4 cup Splenda Granular
> 1/8 teaspoon ground nutmeg
> 1/2 cup crushed ice

In a blender container, combine plums, Diet Mountain Dew, Splenda, and nutmeg. Cover and process on BLEND for 25 seconds. Add ice. Re-cover and process on BLEND for 20 to 25 seconds or until mixture is smooth. Evenly pour into 4 glasses. Serve at once.

Each serving equals:

HE: 1 Fruit • 12 Optional Calories

88 Calories • 0 gm Fat • 0 gm Protein •
22 gm Carbohydrate • 11 mg Sodium •
0 mg Calcium • 2 gm Fiber

DIABETIC EXCHANGES: 1 Fruit

Strawberry Frost Smoothie

I've experimented with both fresh and frozen strawberries, and I've invented some spectacular recipes with each. This time, bring home the reddest, ripest, sweetest berries from the farmer's market—and you'll be rewarded with flavor that can't be topped!

❂ Serves 2 (1 cup)

1 cup sliced fresh strawberries
1 cup cold unsweetened orange juice
2 tablespoons Splenda Granular
1 cup crushed ice

In a blender container, combine strawberries, orange juice, and Splenda. Cover and process on BLEND for 30 seconds. Add ice. Re-cover and process on BLEND for 25 to 30 seconds or until mixture is smooth. Evenly pour into 2 glasses. Serve at once.

Each serving equals:

HE: 1½ Fruit • 6 Optional Calories

80 Calories • 0 gm Fat • 1 gm Protein • 19 gm Carbohydrate • 3 mg Sodium • 21 mg Calcium • 2 gm Fiber

DIABETIC EXCHANGES: 1½ Fruit

Cranberry Orange Smoothie

My friend Barbara loves the blend of orange and cranberry, so this one's for her. From Cape Cod cranberry bogs to the orange groves of sunny Florida, this smoothie surfs the Eastern shores of our great country! ☻ Serves 2 (1¼ cups)

½ cup cold unsweetened orange juice
1 cup cold Ocean Spray reduced-calorie cranberry juice cocktail
2 tablespoons Splenda Granular
1 cup crushed ice

In a blender container, combine orange juice, cranberry juice cocktail, and Splenda. Cover and process on BLEND for 10 seconds. Add ice. Re-cover and process on BLEND for 15 to 20 seconds or until mixture is smooth. Evenly pour into 2 glasses. Serve at once.

Each serving equals:

HE: 1 Fruit • 6 Optional Calories

---

52 Calories • 0 gm Fat • 0 gm Protein •
13 gm Carbohydrate • 5 mg Sodium •
15 mg Calcium • 0 gm Fiber

DIABETIC EXCHANGES: 1 Fruit

Cran-Cot Smoothie

Fresh apricots are undeniably luscious, but they're often hard to get and priced like a luxury item. Canned ones, on the other hand, are readily available, sweet and light, so give them a place of honor in this smoothie and on your pantry shelves!

● Serves 2 (1 cup)

> *1 cup cold Ocean Spray cranberry juice cocktail*
> *1 (8-ounce) can apricots, packed in fruit juice, undrained*
> *2 tablespoons Splenda Granular*
> *1 cup crushed ice*

In a blender container, combine cranberry juice cocktail, undrained apricots, and Splenda. Cover and process on BLEND for 15 seconds. Add ice. Re-cover and process on BLEND for 30 to 35 seconds or until mixture is smooth. Evenly pour into 2 glasses. Serve at once.

Each serving equals:

HE: 1½ Fruit • 6 Optional Calories

84 Calories • 0 gm Fat • 1 gm Protein •
20 gm Carbohydrate • 8 mg Sodium •
24 mg Calcium • 2 gm Fiber

DIABETIC EXCHANGES: 1½ Fruit

Raspberry Fizz Smoothie

In the show-stopping song from *Gypsy,* the star sings "Everything's Coming Up Roses," and this fabulously foamy beverage promises just such happy days ahead!   ☺   Serves 2 (1½ cups)

1½ cups frozen unsweetened red raspberries
½ cup cold unsweetened orange juice
1 cup cold Diet 7-UP
2 tablespoons Splenda Granular
1 cup crushed ice

In a blender container, combine raspberries, orange juice, Diet 7-UP, and Splenda. Cover and process on BLEND for 20 seconds. Add ice. Re-cover and process on BLEND for 15 to 20 seconds or until mixture is smooth. Evenly pour into 2 glasses. Serve at once.

Each serving equals:

HE: 1½ Fruit • 6 Optional Calories

72 Calories • 0 gm Fat • 0 gm Protein •
18 gm Carbohydrate • 18 mg Sodium •
24 mg Calcium • 6 gm Fiber

DIABETIC EXCHANGES: 1 Fruit

Raspberry Ginger Smoothie

This lovely beverage couldn't be easier to prepare or more perfect to serve party guests anytime at all. Celebrate anything and everything, because life is precious!   ❂   Serves 2 (1 cup)

1¼ cups cold diet ginger ale
1½ cups frozen unsweetened red raspberries

In a blender container, combine diet ginger ale and raspberries. Cover and process on BLEND for 30 to 35 seconds or until mixture is smooth. Evenly pour into 2 glasses. Serve at once.

Each serving equals:

HE: 1 Fruit

48 Calories • 0 gm Fat • 1 gm Protein • 11 gm Carbohydrate • 15 mg Sodium • 20 mg Calcium • 6 gm Fiber

DIABETIC EXCHANGES: 1 Fruit

Juicy Fruit Smoothie

It takes a lot of whole fresh fruit to produce even one-half cup of juice, so expect an intensely satisfying flavor experience when you sip this smoothie. It sparkles, it shimmers, and delivers a delectable treat in every mouthful!   ☻   Serves 2 (1½ cups)

½ cup cold unsweetened apple juice
½ cup cold unsweetened orange juice
¼ cup cold Diet Mountain Dew
2 tablespoons Splenda Granular
¼ teaspoon ground cinnamon
1½ cups crushed ice

In a blender container, combine apple juice, orange juice, Diet Mountain Dew, Splenda, and cinnamon. Cover and process on BLEND for 10 seconds. Add ice. Re-cover and process on BLEND for 15 to 20 seconds or until mixture is smooth. Evenly pour into 2 glasses. Serve at once.

Each serving equals:

HE: 1 Fruit • 6 Optional Calories

60 Calories • 0 gm Fat • 0 gm Protein •
15 gm Carbohydrate • 6 mg Sodium •
10 mg Calcium • 0 gm Fiber

DIABETIC EXCHANGES: 1 Fruit

Big Apple Smoothie

It's the city that never sleeps, the town that gives us Broadway shows and wild new fashions. Here's my "hymn" to the lively, lovely, and endlessly energized experience that is New York, New York!

● Serves 2 (1 cup)

1/8 teaspoon ground cinnamon

1 tablespoon Splenda Granular

1 cup cold unsweetened apple juice

1/2 cup unsweetened applesauce

1/4 teaspoon almond extract

1 cup crushed ice

In a small bowl, combine cinnamon and Splenda. Set aside. In a blender container, combine apple juice, applesauce, and almond extract. Cover and process on BLEND for 15 seconds. Add ice. Re-cover and process on BLEND for 20 to 25 seconds or until mixture is smooth. Evenly pour into 2 glasses. Sprinkle half of cinnamon mixture over top of each. Serve at once.

Each serving equals:

HE: 1½ Fruit • 3 Optional Calories

88 Calories • 0 gm Fat • 0 gm Protein • 22 gm Carbohydrate • 5 mg Sodium • 12 mg Calcium • 1 gm Fiber

DIABETIC EXCHANGES: 1½ Fruit

Apple Maple Smoothie

Some marriages were made to last, and the remarkable culinary relationship between apples and maple syrup is one of those—for sure! It's especially good for a Sunday brunch alongside waffles or pancakes, so give it a try. I'm sure my son-in-law, John, would opt for this one!　　　❂　　Serves 2 (1 cup)

> 1 cup cold unsweetened apple juice
> ½ cup (1 small) cored, peeled, and chopped apple
> ¼ cup Log Cabin Sugar Free Maple Syrup
> 1 cup crushed ice

In a blender container, combine apple juice, apple, and maple syrup. Cover and process on BLEND for 15 seconds. Add ice. Recover and process on BLEND for 15 to 20 seconds or until mixture is smooth. Evenly pour into 2 glasses. Serve at once.

Each serving equals:

HE: 1½ Fruit • ¼ Slider

92 Calories • 0 gm Fat • 0 gm Protein •
23 gm Carbohydrate • 54 mg Sodium •
10 mg Calcium • 1 gm Fiber

DIABETIC EXCHANGES: 1½ Fruit

Apple Pie Smoothie

If you've got a hankering for a slice of old-fashioned apple pie but no time to bake and no wish to pile on the fat and calories anyway, here's a sensational substitute that will make you forget what you thought you wanted in the first place! ☻ Serves 2 (1 cup)

1 cup cold unsweetened apple juice
½ cup cold diet ginger ale
1 teaspoon lemon juice
¼ cup Splenda Granular
¼ teaspoon apple pie spice
1 cup crushed ice

In a blender container, combine apple juice, diet ginger ale, lemon juice, Splenda, and apple pie spice. Cover and process on BLEND for 10 seconds. Add ice. Re-cover and process on BLEND for 30 to 35 seconds or until mixture is smooth. Evenly pour into 2 glasses. Serve at once.

Each serving equals:

HE: 1 Fruit • 6 Optional Calories

72 Calories • 0 gm Fat • 0 gm Protein • 18 gm Carbohydrate • 13 mg Sodium • 10 mg Calcium • 0 gm Fiber

DIABETIC EXCHANGES: 1 Fruit

Spiced Grape Smoothie

Are you one of those grown-up kids who always insisted on grape jelly with your peanut butter sandwiches? For some of us, grape is the best of all flavors when it comes to jelly, and to juice. Here's a fresh and fun way to enjoy what you already can't resist!

❍ Serves 2 (1 cup)

> *1 cup cold unsweetened grape juice*
> *¼ cup Splenda Granular*
> *1 tablespoon lemon juice*
> *¼ teaspoon apple pie spice*
> *1 cup crushed ice*

In a blender container, combine grape juice, Splenda, lemon juice, and apple pie spice. Cover and process on BLEND for 15 seconds. Add ice. Re-cover and process on BLEND for 20 to 25 seconds or until mixture is smooth. Evenly pour into 2 glasses. Serve at once.

Each serving equals:

HE: 1 Fruit • 12 Optional Calories

92 Calories • 0 gm Fat • 1 gm Protein •
22 gm Carbohydrate • 4 mg Sodium •
11 mg Calcium • 0 gm Fiber

DIABETIC EXCHANGES: 1½ Fruit

Sparkling Orange Smoothie

I think most of the recipes in this book would make perfect party drinks, but this is one of my grandkids' favorites. If you're planning a birthday celebration and wondering what kind of drinks to serve, why not deliver some healthy vitamin C along with the soda? The kids will never suspect a thing!   ☉   Serves 4 (1 cup)

2 cups cold Diet Mountain Dew
1 (6-ounce) can frozen orange juice concentrate, cut into chunks
1 teaspoon lime juice
½ cup Splenda Granular
1 cup crushed ice

In a blender container, combine Diet Mountain Dew and orange juice concentrate. Cover and process on BLEND for 30 seconds. Add lime juice, Splenda, and ice. Re-cover and process on BLEND for 15 to 20 seconds or until mixture is smooth. Evenly pour into 4 glasses. Serve at once.

Each serving equals:

HE: 1 Fruit

---

76 Calories • 0 gm Fat • 1 gm Protein •
18 gm Carbohydrate • 13 mg Sodium •
14 mg Calcium • 0 gm Fiber

DIABETIC EXCHANGES: 1 Fruit

Chocolate Orange Smoothie

If you've ever tried one of those sliced chocolate "oranges" that blends the irresistible flavor of chocolate with tangy orange, you'll want to put this on your "must-try" list right away. Isn't it amazing how much chocolate flavor a little syrup provides? And it's fat-free!

☻ Serves 2 (1 cup)

> 1 cup cold unsweetened orange juice
> ½ cup cold Diet Mountain Dew
> 2 tablespoons Splenda Granular
> 2 tablespoons Hershey's Lite Chocolate Syrup
> 1 cup crushed ice

In a blender container, combine orange juice, Diet Mountain Dew, Splenda, and chocolate syrup. Cover and process on BLEND for 10 seconds. Add ice. Re-cover and process on BLEND for 15 to 20 seconds or until mixture is smooth. Evenly pour into 2 glasses. Serve at once.

Each serving equals:

HE: 1 Fruit • ¼ Slider • 11 Optional Calories

80 Calories • 0 gm Fat • 1 gm Protein •
19 gm Carbohydrate • 32 mg Sodium •
12 mg Calcium • 0 gm Fiber

DIABETIC EXCHANGES: 1 Fruit

"Moo"-Vable Feasts

Courtesy of our friend the cow, here are calcium-rich and flavor-packed smoothies that feature milk along with wonderful blends of fruit and other flavorings. If you're concerned about getting enough of this healthy mineral, adding a smoothie to your daily menu is a handy option. If your kids aren't great about drinking their milk, don't turn it into a battle; pour it into a blender with some fruit, and win their hearts!

I want to add a few words here about soy milk, which is listed as an alternative to fat-free milk in this section. I've never before suggested it, but I chose to include it this time for two important reasons. I wanted to give people the option of enjoying the potential health benefits that soy products offer, and I wanted to make my recipes available to anyone who is lactose intolerant. I hope this addition to my usual "favorite products" extends the benefits of my Healthy Exchanges lifestyle to even more people!

From apricots to bananas, from berries of all kinds to m-m-marvelous mangos, these smoothies are sure to become family favorites right away!

"Moo"-Vable Feasts

Banana Flip Smoothie

Scrumptious. It's the perfect word to describe the sensual experience of this banana-infused creamy dream! If you've never tried half & half that is remarkably fat free, this is a great way to do so.

☺ Serves 2 (1½ cups)

> *2 cups (2 medium) diced bananas*
> *1 cup cold fat-free milk or soy milk*
> *¼ cup Land O Lakes Fat Free Half & Half*
> *¼ teaspoon almond extract*
> *½ cup crushed ice*

In a blender container, combine banana, milk, half & half, and almond extract. Cover and process on BLEND for 20 seconds. Add ice. Re-cover and process on BLEND for 20 to 25 seconds or until mixture is smooth. Evenly pour into 2 glasses. Serve at once.

Each serving equals:

HE: 2 Fruit • ½ Fat-Free Milk • ¼ Slider

---

180 Calories • 0 gm Fat • 6 gm Protein •
39 gm Carbohydrate • 94 mg Sodium •
208 mg Calcium • 4 gm Fiber

DIABETIC EXCHANGES: 2 Fruit • ½ Fat-Free Milk

Simple Banana Smoothie

Just because something is simple doesn't mean it can't also be truly special. Here's a smoothie for one of those mornings you're so sleepy, all you can do is slice a banana, pour some milk, and spoon a little sweetener into the blender container. Add the crushed ice, and you're done—deliciously so!   ☻   Serves 2 (1 cup)

> 1 cup cold fat-free milk or soy milk
> 1 cup (1 medium) sliced banana
> 2 tablespoons Splenda Granular
> ½ cup crushed ice

In a blender container, combine milk, banana, and Splenda. Cover and process on BLEND for 30 seconds. Add ice. Re-cover and process on BLEND for 15 to 20 seconds or until mixture is smooth. Evenly pour into 2 glasses. Serve at once.

Each serving equals:

HE: 1 Fruit • ½ Fat-Free Milk • 6 Optional Calories

120 Calories • 0 gm Fat • 5 gm Protein •
25 gm Carbohydrate • 64 mg Sodium •
155 mg Calcium • 2 gm Fiber

DIABETIC EXCHANGES: 1 Fruit • ½ Fat-Free Milk

Island Smoothie

Take my advice—the next time canned pineapple is on sale at your favorite market, buy a lot! It's a handy, reliable ingredient for many smoothie recipes, and it's always sweet and good. Skip the tropical cruise and simply sip this smoothie for an instant vacation!

◐ Serves 2 (1½ cups)

> 1 cup cold fat-free milk or soy milk
> 1 (8-ounce) can crushed pineapple, packed in fruit juice, undrained
> 2 tablespoons Splenda Granular
> ½ teaspoon coconut extract
> ¼ teaspoon rum extract
> ½ cup crushed ice

In a blender container, combine milk, undrained pineapple, Splenda, coconut extract, and rum extract. Cover and process on BLEND for 20 seconds. Add ice. Re-cover and process on BLEND for 20 to 25 seconds or until mixture is smooth. Evenly pour into 2 glasses. Serve at once.

Each serving equals:

HE: 1 Fruit • ½ Fat-Free Milk • 6 Optional Calories

88 Calories • 0 gm Fat • 5 gm Protein • 17 gm Carbohydrate • 65 mg Sodium • 168 mg Calcium • 1 gm Fiber

DIABETIC EXCHANGES: 1 Fruit • ½ Fat-Free Milk

Fresh Strawberry Milk Smoothie

I almost always use a bit of lemon juice when I make a strawberry dish using fresh berries—the bit of citric acid brings out the sweetness of the berries. This is one of my favorite no-stress beverages. It's quick, it features my favorite berry, and it's a great way to celebrate my very own strawberry patch!

○ Serves 2 (1½ cups)

> 1 cup cold fat-free milk or soy milk
> 2 cups fresh sliced strawberries
> 2 tablespoons Splenda Granular
> 1 teaspoon lemon juice
> 1 cup crushed ice

In a blender container, combine milk, strawberries, Splenda, and lemon juice. Cover and process on BLEND for 15 seconds. Add ice. Re-cover and process on BLEND for 15 to 20 seconds or until mixture is smooth. Evenly pour into 2 glasses. Serve at once.

Each serving equals:

HE: 1 Fruit • ½ Fat-Free Milk • 6 Optional Calories

96 Calories • 0 gm Fat • 5 gm Protein •
19 gm Carbohydrate • 65 mg Sodium •
162 mg Calcium • 3 gm Fiber

DIABETIC EXCHANGES: 1 Fruit • ½ Fat-Free Milk

Berry Mint Smoothie

If the combination of mint and strawberry seems a bit unusual to you, you're not alone. Cliff looked a little shocked when I told him what he'd be tasting. But he agreed with me that the two flavors bring out the best in each other and offer a terrific contrast of cool and sweet.   ☽   Serves 2 (1¼ cups)

> 1 cup cold fat-free milk or soy milk
> ¼ cup Land O Lakes Fat Free Half & Half
> ¼ cup Splenda Granular
> ⅛ teaspoon mint extract
> 1½ cups frozen unsweetened strawberries

In a blender container, combine milk, half & half, Splenda, and mint extract. Cover and process on BLEND for 15 seconds. Add strawberries. Re-cover and process on BLEND for 20 to 25 seconds or until mixture is smooth. Evenly pour into 2 glasses. Serve at once.

Each serving equals:

HE: ¾ Fruit • ½ Fat-Free Milk • ¼ Slider • 6 Optional Calories

108 Calories • 0 gm Fat • 6 gm Protein • 21 gm Carbohydrate • 96 mg Sodium • 216 mg Calcium • 2 gm Fiber

DIABETIC EXCHANGES: ½ Fruit • ½ Fat-Free Milk

Blueberry Bliss Smoothie

What is bliss? Happiness, joy, a sense that everything is right with the world. If you haven't experienced much bliss recently, maybe it's time to seek it out in a tall, cool glass that is as good for the soul as it is for your bones!   ☺   Serves 2 (1½ cups)

1 cup cold fat-free milk or soy milk
¼ cup Land O Lakes Fat Free Half & Half
2 tablespoons Splenda Granular
¼ teaspoon coconut extract
1½ cups frozen unsweetened blueberries
2 teaspoons flaked coconut

In a blender container, combine milk, half & half, Splenda, and coconut extract. Cover and process on BLEND for 20 seconds. Add blueberries. Re-cover and process on BLEND for 20 to 25 seconds or until mixture is smooth. Evenly pour into 2 glasses. Sprinkle 1 teaspoon coconut over top of each. Serve at once.

Each serving equals:

HE: 1 Fruit • ½ Fat-Free Milk • 8 Optional Calories

129 Calories • 1 gm Fat • 6 gm Protein •
24 gm Carbohydrate • 99 mg Sodium •
208 mg Calcium • 3 gm Fiber

DIABETIC EXCHANGES: 1 Fruit • ½ Fat-Free Milk

Creamy Raspberry Smoothie

Even if you don't love the taste of milk made with dry milk powder, you'll soon become a fan of its culinary magic in recipes like this one. Along with the half & half, it makes a tasty shake super-duper rich and satisfying. ☻ Serves 2 (1 cup)

⅔ cup Carnation Nonfat Dry Milk Powder
1 cup cold water
2 tablespoons Land O Lakes Fat Free Half & Half
2 tablespoons Splenda Granular
1½ cups frozen unsweetened red raspberries

In a blender container, combine dry milk powder, water, half & half, and Splenda. Cover and process on BLEND for 10 seconds. Add raspberries. Re-cover and process on BLEND for 25 to 30 seconds or until mixture is smooth. Evenly pour into 2 glasses. Serve at once.

Each serving equals:

HE: 1 Fat-Free Milk • 1 Fruit • 16 Optional Calories

136 Calories • 0 gm Fat • 9 gm Protein •
25 gm Carbohydrate • 143 mg Sodium •
345 mg Calcium • 6 gm Fiber

DIABETIC EXCHANGES: 1 Fat-Free Milk • 1 Fruit

Razzamatazz Smoothie

I have a whole shelf of extracts in my kitchen cabinet, and almond is one of my favorite choices to add taste appeal to a dish already pretty wonderful on its own. Here, it adds a silken luxury that is truly yummy! ☻ Serves 2 (1 full cup)

> 1 cup cold fat-free milk or soy milk
> ¼ cup Land O Lakes Fat Free Half & Half
> 2 tablespoons Splenda Granular
> ¼ teaspoon almond extract
> 1½ cups frozen unsweetened red raspberries

In a blender container, combine milk, half & half, Splenda, and almond extract. Cover and process on BLEND for 15 seconds. Add raspberries. Re-cover and process on BLEND for 20 to 25 seconds or until mixture is smooth. Evenly pour into 2 glasses. Serve at once.

Each serving equals:

HE: 1 Fruit • ½ Fat-Free Milk • ¼ Slider •
6 Optional Calories

---

108 Calories • 0 gm Fat • 6 gm Protein •
21 gm Carbohydrate • 94 mg Sodium •
219 mg Calcium • 6 gm Fiber

DIABETIC EXCHANGES: 1 Fruit • ½ Fat-Free Milk

Raspberry Froth Smoothie

I like the pretty foam on the top of blender drinks but it's a challenge to get it to taste delicious, not like just so much pink air. I put on my scientist's cap along with my sensible chef's hat to figure this one out, and I think I got it with the combo of gelatin and evaporated milk! ☺ Serves 4 (1 full cup)

> 1 (4-serving) package JELL-O sugar-free raspberry gelatin
> ½ cup boiling water
> 3 cups frozen unsweetened red raspberries
> 1 (12-fluid-ounce) can Carnation Evaporated Fat Free Milk
> ¾ cup crushed ice

In a blender container, combine dry gelatin and boiling water. Cover and process on BLEND until gelatin is dissolved. Add raspberries, evaporated milk, and ice. Re-cover and process on BLEND for 20 to 25 seconds or until mixture is smooth. Evenly pour into 4 glasses. Serve at once.

Each serving equals:

HE: 1 Fruit • ¾ Fat-Free Milk • 10 Optional Calories

---

116 Calories • 0 gm Fat • 7 gm Protein •
22 gm Carbohydrate • 125 mg Sodium •
260 mg Calcium • 6 gm Fiber

DIABETIC EXCHANGES: 1 Fruit • 1 Fat-Free Milk

Uptown Peach Smoothie

I'm just "nuts" about this one, which tempts the palate by persuading some sweet peaches to hold hands with the sumptuous flavor of almonds times two. It satisfies heart and soul all at once, don't you think?　　❍　　Serves 2 (full 1½ cups)

> 1 cup cold fat-free milk or soy milk
> 1 (8-ounce) can sliced peaches, packed in fruit juice, undrained
> ½ teaspoon almond extract
> 1 cup crushed ice
> 2 tablespoons Cool Whip Lite
> 2 teaspoons finely chopped slivered almonds

In a blender container, combine milk, undrained peaches, and almond extract. Cover and process on BLEND for 20 seconds. Add ice. Re-cover and process on BLEND for 25 to 30 seconds or until mixture is smooth. Evenly pour into 2 glasses. Top each glass with 1 tablespoon Cool Whip Lite and 1 teaspoon almonds. Serve at once.

Each serving equals:

HE: 1 Fruit • ½ Fat-Free Milk • ¼ Fat •
17 Optional Calories

138 Calories • 2 gm Fat • 5 gm Protein •
25 gm Carbohydrate • 82 mg Sodium •
161 mg Calcium • 1 gm Fiber

DIABETIC EXCHANGES: 1 Fruit • ½ Fat-Free Milk

Peach Isle Smoothie

When I taste a hint of coconut in a recipe, I'm transported in an instant to a world of relaxation and warmth—that's the power in one tasty tropical nut! Here, it's the catalyst for a creamy peach beverage that is as soothing as it is oh-so-sweet.

◐ Serves 2 (full 1½ cups)

> 1½ cups cold fat-free milk or soy milk
> ¼ cup Splenda Granular
> ¼ teaspoon coconut extract
> 1 cup frozen unsweetened sliced peaches

In a blender container, combine milk, Splenda, coconut extract, and peaches. Cover and process on BLEND for 45 to 60 seconds or until mixture is smooth. Evenly pour into 2 glasses. Serve at once.

Each serving equals:

HE: 1 Fruit • ¾ Fat-Free Milk • 12 Optional Calories

120 Calories • 0 gm Fat • 9 gm Protein • 21 gm Carbohydrate • 127 mg Sodium • 229 mg Calcium • 2 gm Fiber

DIABETIC EXCHANGES: 1 Fruit • 1 Fat-Free Milk

Peach Splash Smoothie

Are you lucky enough to have a peach tree on your property, and an abundant harvest of fresh peaches every summer? Lucky you! I hope you also have a nice big freezer that will allow you to enjoy that sensational peach flavor all year long. The rest of us can buy up bushels fresh from the farm and freeze them ourselves—or simply use the best frozen peaches we can find at the store.

◐ Serves 2 (full 1 cup)

> 1½ cups cold fat-free milk or soy milk
> ¼ cup Splenda Granular
> ¼ teaspoon ground cinnamon
> 1½ cups frozen sliced unsweetened peaches
> 2 tablespoons Cool Whip Lite

In a blender container, combine milk, Splenda, and cinnamon. Cover and process on BLEND for 10 seconds. Add peaches. Re-cover and process on BLEND for 30 to 35 seconds or until mixture is smooth. Evenly pour into 2 glasses and garnish each with 1 table-spoon Cool Whip Lite. Serve at once.

Each serving equals:

HE: 1½ Fruit • ¾ Fat-Free Milk • ¼ Slider • 2 Optional Calories

136 Calories • 0 gm Fat • 5 gm Protein • 29 gm Carbohydrate • 64 mg Sodium • 237 mg Calcium • 2 gm Fiber

DIABETIC EXCHANGES: 1½ Fruit • 1 Fat-Free Milk

Peaches & Cream Smoothie

Here's another "pantry pleaser," one of those recipes that lets you enjoy a fresh fruit smoothie even when there isn't a sliver of fresh fruit for miles! If you've got canned fruit on the shelf, you can make a splendid treat anytime—and that's got to feel good!

◐ Serves 2 (1½ cups)

1 (16-ounce) can peaches, packed in fruit juice, undrained
2 tablespoons Splenda Granular
1 cup cold fat-free milk or soy milk
¼ cup Land O Lakes Fat Free Half & Half
1 cup crushed ice

In a blender container, combine undrained peaches and Splenda. Cover and process on BLEND for 15 seconds. Add milk, half & half, and ice. Re-cover and process on BLEND for 30 to 35 seconds or until mixture is smooth. Evenly pour into 2 glasses. Serve at once.

Each serving equals:

HE: 2 Fruit • ½ Fat-Free Milk • ¼ Slider • 6 Optional Calories

176 Calories • 0 gm Fat • 5 gm Protein •
39 gm Carbohydrate • 129 mg Sodium •
199 mg Calcium • 1 gm Fiber

DIABETIC EXCHANGES: 2 Fruit • ½ Fat-Free Milk

Peachy Keen Smoothie

I get questions from time to time about using lemon juice in recipes. Fresh lemon juice is considered the tastiest, if you have a spare lemon on hand. (Always roll your lemon a few times before squeezing to get the most juice from it!) Otherwise, one of those little plastic lemons can do the trick in this recipe and others.

◐ Serves 2 (1½ cups)

> 1½ cups (3 medium) peeled and sliced fresh peaches
> 1 cup cold fat-free milk or soy milk
> 2 tablespoons Splenda Granular
> 2 teaspoons lemon juice
> ½ cup crushed ice

In a blender container, combine peaches, milk, and Splenda. Cover and process on BLEND for 20 seconds. Add lemon juice and ice. Re-cover and process on BLEND for 15 to 20 seconds or until mixture is smooth. Evenly pour into 2 glasses. Serve at once.

Each serving equals:

HE: 1½ Fruit • ½ Fat-Free Milk • 6 Optional Calories

108 Calories • 0 gm Fat • 5 gm Protein •
22 gm Carbohydrate • 64 mg Sodium •
157 mg Calcium • 2 gm Fiber

DIABETIC EXCHANGES: 1½ Fruit • ½ Fat-Free Milk

Abram's Apricot Smoothie

Smoothies are a great way to nourish your kids, especially if you find yourself with a picky eater and you're concerned that he or she is consuming enough nutrients. But they're also kid-pleasing just because they come in such pretty colors and they taste so good! My grandson Abram gave this smoothie a perfect ten.

○ Serves 2 (1 cup)

> 1 cup cold fat-free milk or soy milk
> 1 (8-ounce) can apricots, packed in fruit juice, undrained
> 2 tablespoons Splenda Granular
> ½ teaspoon vanilla extract
> ½ cup crushed ice

In a blender container, combine milk, undrained apricots, Splenda, and vanilla extract. Cover and process on BLEND for 30 seconds. Add ice. Re-cover and process on BLEND for 15 to 20 seconds or until mixture is smooth. Evenly pour into 2 glasses. Serve at once.

Each serving equals:

HE: 1 Fruit • ½ Fat-Free Milk • 6 Optional Calories

---

104 Calories • 0 gm Fat • 5 gm Protein •
21 gm Carbohydrate • 68 mg Sodium •
164 mg Calcium • 2 gm Fiber

DIABETIC EXCHANGES: 1 Fruit • ½ Fat-Free Milk

Coconut Apricot Smoothie

If you want to know what temptation tastes like, here's a great example: a silken blend of apricots and coconut just packed with pleasure. It's delectably cool and creamy.

❂ Serves 2 (2 cups)

> 1 cup cold fat-free milk or soy milk
> 1 (8-ounce) can apricots, packed in fruit juice, undrained
> 1 tablespoon Splenda Granular
> ½ teaspoon coconut extract
> 1 cup crushed ice
> 2 tablespoons Cool Whip Lite
> 1 teaspoon flaked coconut

In a blender container, combine milk, undrained apricots, Splenda, and coconut extract. Cover and process on BLEND for 20 seconds. Add ice. Re-cover and process on BLEND for 30 to 35 seconds or until mixture is smooth. Evenly pour into 2 glasses and garnish each with 1 tablespoon Cool Whip Lite and ½ teaspoon coconut. Serve at once.

Each serving equals:

HE: 1 Fruit • ½ Fat-Free Milk • 17 Optional Calories

117 Calories • 1 gm Fat • 5 gm Protein •
22 gm Carbohydrate • 70 mg Sodium •
164 mg Calcium • 2 gm Fiber

DIABETIC EXCHANGES: 1 Fruit • ½ Fat-Free Milk

Apricot Chill Smoothie

I'm a big fan of taking something good and making it better, better, and better still. A rich and luscious beverage is made more luscious and lip-smacking with just a bit of half & half. Wow!

● Serves 2 (1¼ cups)

> 1 (8-ounce) can apricot halves, packed in fruit juice, undrained
> 1 cup cold fat-free milk or soy milk
> ¼ cup Land O Lakes Fat Free Half & Half
> 2 tablespoons Splenda Granular
> ½ teaspoon coconut extract
> ½ cup crushed ice

In a blender container, combine undrained apricots, milk, half & half, Splenda, and coconut extract. Cover and process on BLEND for 20 seconds. Add ice. Re-cover and process on BLEND for 20 to 25 seconds or until mixture is smooth. Evenly pour into 2 glasses. Serve at once.

Each serving equals:

HE: 1 Fruit • ½ Fat-Free Milk • ¼ Slider • 6 Optional Calories

---

120 Calories • 0 gm Fat • 6 gm Protein •
24 gm Carbohydrate • 98 mg Sodium •
212 mg Calcium • 2 gm Fiber

DIABETIC EXCHANGES: 1 Fruit • ½ Fat-Free Milk

Mango Coconut Smoothie

If you're not sure what a ripe mango feels and smells like, ask your grocer for help in picking the best of the batch. You'll soon get the hang of selecting fruit that is really ripe—an important skill to develop in becoming a smoothie superstar chef!

❍ Serves 2 (1 cup)

1 cup (2 medium) peeled and diced fresh ripe mango
1 cup cold fat-free milk or soy milk
2 tablespoons Land O Lakes Fat Free Half & Half
2 tablespoons Splenda Granular
½ teaspoon coconut extract

In a blender container, combine mango, milk, half & half, Splenda, and coconut extract. Cover and process on BLEND for 20 to 25 seconds or until mixture is smooth. Evenly pour into 2 glasses. Serve at once.

HINT: 1 cup canned diced mango, drained, may be used in place of fresh mango.

Each serving equals:

HE: 1 Fruit • ½ Fat-Free Milk • 10 Optional Calories

108 Calories • 0 gm Fat • 5 gm Protein •
22 gm Carbohydrate • 89 mg Sodium •
177 mg Calcium • 1 gm Fiber

DIABETIC EXCHANGES: 1 Fruit • ½ Fat-Free Milk

Orange Glow Smoothie

Double your pleasure and double your fun when you double up on flavor ingredients, as I have in this orangy delight! By using both juice and fruit, you rev up your smoothie and delectably deepen the taste.   ☻   Serves 2 (1 cup)

> ½ cup cold fat-free milk or soy milk
> ½ cup cold unsweetened orange juice
> 1 (11-ounce) can mandarin oranges, rinsed and drained
> 2 tablespoons Splenda Granular
> 1 cup crushed ice

In a blender container, combine milk, orange juice, mandarin oranges, and Splenda. Cover and process on BLEND for 20 seconds. Add ice. Re-cover and process on BLEND for 15 to 20 seconds or until mixture is smooth. Evenly pour into 2 glasses. Serve at once.

Each serving equals:

HE: 1½ Fruit • ¼ Fat-Free Milk • 6 Optional Calories

120 Calories • 0 gm Fat • 2 gm Protein •
28 gm Carbohydrate • 42 mg Sodium •
80 mg Calcium • 0 gm Fiber

DIABETIC EXCHANGES: 1½ Fruit

Orange Coconut Smoothie

I get my ideas in many different ways, and this one took some of its inspiration from a holiday treat—an orange-tinted, coconut-covered Halloween delight. Be careful to find all the seeds when you section the orange—chopped-up seeds add a bitter taste you definitely don't want!   ☻   Serves 2 (1¼ cups)

½ cup cold Diet Mountain Dew
½ cup cold unsweetened orange juice
⅔ cup Carnation Nonfat Dry Milk Powder
1 (medium-sized) orange, peeled, seeded, and sectioned
½ teaspoon coconut extract
1 cup crushed ice

In a blender container, combine Diet Mountain Dew, orange juice, and dry milk powder. Cover and process on BLEND for 10 seconds. Add orange slices, coconut extract, and ice. Re-cover and process on BLEND for 20 to 25 seconds or until mixture is smooth. Evenly pour into 2 glasses. Serve at once.

Each serving equals:

HE: 1 Fat-Free Milk • 1 Fruit

124 Calories • 0 gm Fat • 9 gm Protein •
22 gm Carbohydrate • 132 mg Sodium •
319 mg Calcium • 1 gm Fiber

DIABETIC EXCHANGES: 1 Fat-Free Milk • 1 Fruit

Orange Jubilee Smoothie

I could have named this smoothie after that beloved ice cream treat, the creamsicle, which also celebrates the joys of orange and creamy goodness. The first version of this didn't include the vanilla, but in the final version it made such a great difference!

◐ Serves 4 (1 cup)

> 1 (6-ounce) can frozen orange juice concentrate, thawed
> 2 cups cold fat-free milk or soy milk
> ¼ cup Splenda Granular
> 1 teaspoon vanilla extract
> 1 cup crushed ice

In a blender container, combine thawed orange juice concentrate, milk, Splenda, and vanilla extract. Cover and process on BLEND for 30 seconds. Add ice. Re-cover and process on BLEND for 30 to 35 seconds or until mixture is smooth. Evenly pour into 4 glasses. Serve at once.

Each serving equals:

HE: 1 Fruit • ½ Fat-Free Milk • 6 Optional Calories

116 Calories • 0 gm Fat • 5 gm Protein •
24 gm Carbohydrate • 65 mg Sodium •
164 mg Calcium • 0 gm Fiber

DIABETIC EXCHANGES: 1 Fruit • ½ Fat-Free Milk

Limeade Smoothie

Yes, you could certainly serve this on St. Paddy's Day, but I don't believe in saving all green food and drink for one day a year! The soft shade of green of this smoothie just hints at the enticing lushness of its down-the-throat pleasure.

☻ Serves 4 (1 full cup)

> 1 (6-ounce) can frozen limeade concentrate
> 1 (12-fluid-ounce) can Carnation Evaporated Fat Free Milk
> ½ cup cold Diet Mountain Dew
> ¼ cup Splenda Granular
> 6 to 8 drops green food coloring
> 3 cups crushed ice

Coarsely chop limeade concentrate, using a sharp knife. In a blender container, combine chopped limeade concentrate, evaporated milk, Diet Mountain Dew, Splenda, and green food coloring. Cover and process on BLEND for 15 seconds. Add ice. Recover and process on BLEND for 30 to 35 seconds or until mixture is smooth. Evenly pour into 4 glasses. Serve at once.

Each serving equals:

HE: 1 Fruit • ¾ Fat-Free Milk • 6 Optional Calories

---

160 Calories • 0 gm Fat • 6 gm Protein •
34 gm Carbohydrate • 126 mg Sodium •
242 mg Calcium • 0 gm Fiber

DIABETIC EXCHANGES: 1 Fruit • 1 Fat-Free Milk

Garden of Eden Smoothie

I have often joked over the years that if I'd been Adam, I'd have passed Eve and her apple right by in favor of the nearest strawberry patch! But perhaps it's time to rethink my little bit of humor by combining the two into something resembling paradise on the palate.　　❍　　Serves 2 (1½ cups)

> 1 cup cold fat-free milk or soy milk
> 1 cup cold unsweetened apple juice
> 2 tablespoons Splenda Granular
> 1 cup frozen unsweetened strawberries

In a blender container, combine milk, apple juice, and Splenda. Cover and process on BLEND for 10 seconds. Add strawberries. Re-cover and process on BLEND for 30 to 40 seconds or until mixture is smooth. Evenly pour into 2 glasses. Serve at once.

Each serving equals:

HE: 1½ Fruit • ½ Fat-Free Milk • 6 Optional Calories

148 Calories • 0 gm Fat • 5 gm Protein •
32 gm Carbohydrate • 69 mg Sodium •
177 mg Calcium • 2 gm Fiber

DIABETIC EXCHANGES: 1½ Fruit • ½ Fat-Free Milk

Strawberry Creamsicle Smoothie

Don't they say you can never be too rich or too thin? Well, we know you can actually be too thin, but when it comes to smoothies, too rich is not a problem but an opportunity for mouthwatering delight! ☻ Serves 4 (1¼ cups)

½ cup cold unsweetened orange juice

1 (12-fluid-ounce) can Carnation Evaporated Fat Free Milk

2 cups frozen unsweetened whole strawberries

1 (4-serving) package JELL-O sugar-free strawberry gelatin

In a blender container, combine orange juice and evaporated milk. Cover and process on BLEND for 10 seconds. Add strawberries and dry gelatin. Re-cover and process on BLEND for 30 to 40 seconds or until mixture is smooth. Evenly pour into 4 glasses. Serve at once.

Each serving equals:

HE: ¾ Fat-Free Milk • ¾ Fruit • 10 Optional Calories

128 Calories • 0 gm Fat • 7 gm Protein •
25 gm Carbohydrate • 128 mg Sodium •
260 mg Calcium • 2 gm Fiber

DIABETIC EXCHANGES: 1 Fat-Free Milk • 1 Fruit

Strawberry Colada Smoothie

Most people think that piña or strawberry coladas require rum to make them "authentic," but believe me, this beautiful blend needs nothing more than milk and sweet fruit to win your heart! Try it for Valentine's Day, and love will abide.   ☻   Serves 2 (1½ cups)

> 1 (8-ounce) can crushed pineapple, packed in fruit juice,
>   undrained
> 1 cup cold fat-free milk or soy milk
> 2 tablespoons Splenda Granular
> ½ teaspoon coconut extract
> 1 cup frozen unsweetened strawberries

In a blender container, combine undrained pineapple, milk, Splenda, and coconut extract. Cover and process on BLEND for 15 seconds. Add strawberries. Re-cover and process on BLEND for 45 to 60 seconds or until mixture is smooth. Evenly pour into 2 glasses. Serve at once.

Each serving equals:

HE: 1½ Fruit • ½ Fat-Free Milk • 6 Optional Calories

124 Calories • 0 gm Fat • 4 gm Protein •
27 gm Carbohydrate • 67 mg Sodium •
185 mg Calcium • 3 gm Fiber

DIABETIC EXCHANGES: 1½ Fruit • ½ Fat-Free Milk

Pineapple Colada Smoothie

Here's a fantastic party drink that family and friends will just adore! It's light, fruity, and creamy, perfect for a celebration of anything at all!   ☻   Serves 2 (1½ cups)

> 1 cup cold fat-free milk or soy milk
> 1 (8-ounce) can crushed pineapple, packed in fruit juice,
>   undrained
> ¼ cup cold unsweetened orange juice
> 2 tablespoons Splenda Granular
> ½ teaspoon coconut extract

In a blender container, combine milk, undrained pineapple, orange juice, Splenda, and coconut extract. Cover and process on BLEND for 30 to 35 seconds or until mixture is smooth. Evenly pour into 2 glasses. Serve at once.

Each serving equals:

HE: 1¼ Fruit • ½ Fat-Free Milk • 6 Optional Calories

100 Calories • 0 gm Fat • 5 gm Protein •
20 gm Carbohydrate • 65 mg Sodium •
170 mg Calcium • 1 gm Fiber

DIABETIC EXCHANGES: 1 Fruit • ½ Fat-Free Milk

Bali Hai Banana Smoothie

One of the prettiest songs in the great old musical *South Pacific* is the one that sings the praises of the island of Bali Hai, where the girls are exquisite, the moon never looked bigger or more beautiful, and love is sure to find you. Here's what all those pretty girls and handsome G.I.s were probably drinking!

◑ Serves 2 (1½ cups)

> 1 cup (1 medium) diced banana
> 1 (8-ounce) can crushed pineapple, packed in fruit juice, undrained
> 1 cup cold fat-free milk or soy milk
> 2 tablespoons Splenda Granular
> ¼ teaspoon rum extract
> 1 cup crushed ice

In a blender container, combine banana, undrained pineapple, milk, Splenda, and rum extract. Cover and process on BLEND for 15 seconds. Add ice. Re-cover and process on BLEND for 15 to 20 seconds or until mixture is smooth. Evenly pour into 2 glasses. Serve at once.

Each serving equals:

HE: 2 Fruit • ½ Fat-Free Milk • 6 Optional Calories

---

152 Calories • 0 gm Fat • 6 gm Protein •
32 gm Carbohydrate • 66 mg Sodium •
176 mg Calcium • 2 gm Fiber

DIABETIC EXCHANGES: 2 Fruit • ½ Fat-Free Milk

Banana Berry Smoothie

You'll notice that you don't need extra ice in this recipe and many others, because the frozen fruit chunks provide the same thickening power that crushed ice does—hurray! The result is thick and rich and oh-so-luscious! ☻ Serves 4 (1¼ cups)

> 1 (8-ounce) can crushed pineapple, packed in fruit juice,
>   undrained
> 1 cup (1 medium) sliced banana
> 2 cups cold fat-free milk or soy milk
> 2 cups frozen unsweetened strawberries

In a blender container, combine undrained pineapple, banana, and milk. Cover and process on BLEND for 20 seconds. Add strawberries. Re-cover and process on BLEND for 20 to 25 seconds or until mixture is smooth. Evenly pour into 4 glasses. Serve at once.

Each serving equals:

HE: 1½ Fruit • ½ Fat-Free Milk

136 Calories • 0 gm Fat • 5 gm Protein •
29 gm Carbohydrate • 71 mg Sodium •
175 mg Calcium • 4 gm Fiber

DIABETIC EXCHANGES: 1½ Fruit • ½ Fat-Free Milk

Hawaiian Pleasure Smoothie

Want the luxurious fun of a luau without leaving home tonight? You can play "Let's Pretend We're in Maui" while you're watching your favorite TV shows and sipping this.

☻ Serves 4 (1 cup)

> 1 (8-ounce) can crushed pineapple, packed in fruit juice, undrained
> 1 cup cold Diet Mountain Dew
> ⅔ cup Carnation Nonfat Dry Milk Powder
> 2 tablespoons Splenda Granular
> 1 cup (1 medium) diced banana
> 1 cup frozen unsweetened strawberries
> 4 tablespoons Cool Whip Lite
> 4 teaspoons flaked coconut

In a blender container, combine undrained pineapple, Diet Mountain Dew, dry milk powder, and Splenda. Cover and process on BLEND for 10 seconds. Add banana and strawberries. Re-cover and process on BLEND for 30 to 35 seconds or until mixture is smooth. For each serving, pour 1 cup mixture into a glass and top with 1 tablespoon Cool Whip Lite and 1 teaspoon coconut. Serve at once.

Each serving equals:

HE: 1¼ Fruit • ½ Fat-Free Milk • 19 Optional Calories

137 Calories • 1 gm Fat • 5 gm Protein •
27 gm Carbohydrate • 69 mg Sodium •
170 mg Calcium • 2 gm Fiber

DIABETIC EXCHANGES: 1 Fruit • ½ Fat-Free Milk

Pink Hurricane Smoothie

Want to be swept away on a velvety pink cloud? It does sound delightful, doesn't it? I've always loved pink drinks, whether the berry of choice is strawberry or raspberry.

◐ Serves 2 (1½ cups)

> 1 cup cold fat-free milk or soy milk
> 1 cup (1 medium) diced banana
> 2 tablespoons Splenda Granular
> ¼ teaspoon almond extract
> ¾ cup frozen unsweetened red raspberries
> ½ cup crushed ice

In a blender container, combine milk, banana, Splenda, and almond extract. Cover and process on BLEND for 10 seconds. Add raspberries and ice. Re-cover and process on BLEND for 15 to 20 seconds or until mixture is smooth. Evenly pour into 2 glasses. Serve at once.

Each serving equals:

HE: 1½ Fruit • ½ Fat-Free Milk • 6 Optional Calories

140 Calories • 0 gm Fat • 5 gm Protein •
30 gm Carbohydrate • 64 mg Sodium •
165 mg Calcium • 5 gm Fiber

DIABETIC EXCHANGES: 1½ Fruit • ½ Fat-Free Milk

Raspberry Banana Smoothie

Let me tempt you today with a scrumptious combination that is snazzy enough to share the table with your best china and crystal (or whatever you've got, of course!). ◐ Serves 2 (1½ cups)

1 cup cold fat-free milk or soy milk
1 cup (1 medium) diced banana
2 tablespoons Splenda Granular
¾ cup frozen unsweetened red raspberries

In a blender container, combine milk, banana, and Splenda. Cover and process on BLEND for 15 seconds. Add raspberries. Re-cover and process on BLEND for 15 to 20 seconds or until mixture is smooth. Evenly pour into 2 glasses. Serve at once.

Each serving equals:

HE: 1½ Fruit • ½ Fat-Free Milk • 6 Optional Calories

140 Calories • 0 gm Fat • 5 gm Protein •
30 gm Carbohydrate • 64 mg Sodium •
165 mg Calcium • 5 gm Fiber

DIABETIC EXCHANGES: 1½ Fruit • ½ Fat-Free Milk

Blueberry Banana Smoothie

Blueberries turn this smoothie into a sensational pale purple, while the banana helps make it irresistibly rich and filling. When you've got no time for breakfast, make your own creamy drink and take it on the road!   ❂   Serves 2 (1 cup)

> 1 cup cold fat-free milk or soy milk
> 2 tablespoons Splenda Granular
> ¾ cup frozen unsweetened blueberries
> 1 cup (1 medium) diced banana

In a blender container, combine milk, Splenda, blueberries, and banana. Cover and process on BLEND for 15 to 20 seconds or until mixture is smooth. Evenly pour into 2 glasses. Serve at once.

Each serving equals:

HE: 1½ Fruit • ½ Fat-Free Milk • 6 Optional Calories

148 Calories • 0 gm Fat • 5 gm Protein •
32 gm Carbohydrate • 65 mg Sodium •
160 mg Calcium • 3 gm Fiber

DIABETIC EXCHANGES: 1½ Fruit • ½ Fat-Free Milk

Sweet Cherry Banana Smoothie

Cherries have a short summer season but the memory of their special sweetness lasts all year long, especially thanks to the great folks who freeze the cream of the crop for our pleasure in the cold months to come. This one is for my son James, who chooses cherries over other fruits. ☾ Serves 2 (1½ cups)

> 1 cup (1 medium) diced banana
> 1 cup frozen unsweetened bing or sweet cherries
> 1 cup cold fat-free milk or soy milk

In a blender container, combine banana, cherries, and milk. Cover and process on BLEND for 20 to 25 seconds or until mixture is smooth. Evenly pour into 2 glasses. Serve at once.

Each serving equals:

HE: 2 Fruit • ½ Fat-Free Milk

164 Calories • 0 gm Fat • 6 gm Protein •
35 gm Carbohydrate • 64 mg Sodium •
166 mg Calcium • 3 gm Fiber

DIABETIC EXCHANGES: 2 Fruit • ½ Fat-Free Milk

Creamy Apricot Banana Smoothie

When a sweetly dense fruit like apricots are ground up in the blender, they help to thicken and "inflate" the drink, just as bananas do. This luscious blend is a wonderful addition to a summer brunch on the patio. ☻ Serves 2 (1¼ cups)

1 (8-ounce) can apricot halves, packed in fruit juice, undrained
1 cup (1 medium) diced banana
1 cup cold fat-free milk or soy milk
2 tablespoons Splenda Granular

In a blender container, combine undrained apricots, banana, milk, and Splenda. Cover and process on BLEND for 30 to 35 seconds or until mixture is smooth. Evenly pour into 2 glasses. Serve at once.

Each serving equals:

HE: 2 Fruit • ½ Fat-Free Milk • 6 Optional Calories

172 Calories • 0 gm Fat • 5 gm Protein •
38 gm Carbohydrate • 69 mg Sodium •
169 mg Calcium • 3 gm Fiber

DIABETIC EXCHANGES: 2 Fruit • ½ Fat-Free Milk

Blushing Peach Smoothie

We won't embarrass the peach by singing its praises too loudly, but the raspberries blended with it will surely pinken its pale orange color to the irresistible pink of a blush. Mmmm!

◐ Serves 4 (1 cup)

1 (8-ounce) can sliced peaches, packed in fruit juice, undrained
1 cup (1 medium) sliced banana
1 cup cold fat-free milk or soy milk
2 tablespoons Splenda Granular
¼ teaspoon coconut extract
1½ cups frozen unsweetened red raspberries
Mint sprigs, optional

In a blender container, combine undrained peaches, banana, milk, Splenda, and coconut extract. Cover and process on BLEND for 20 seconds. Add raspberries. Re-cover and process on BLEND for 20 to 25 seconds or until mixture is smooth. Evenly pour into 4 glasses. Garnish each glass with a mint sprig, if desired. Serve at once.

Each serving equals:

HE: 1½ Fruit • ¼ Fat-Free Milk • 3 Optional Calories

112 Calories • 0 gm Fat • 3 gm Protein •
25 gm Carbohydrate • 41 mg Sodium •
84 mg Calcium • 2 gm Fiber

DIABETIC EXCHANGES: 2 Fruit

Pink Peach Smoothie

The exquisite shades of a summer sunset make this blend one that is a must-have on any July or August menu. It's a scrumptious combination of sweetness and lush texture, perfect for entertaining but just right for a party of two.   ☾   Serves 2 (1¼ cups)

> 1 cup cold fat-free milk or soy milk
> 2 tablespoons Land O Lakes Fat Free Half & Half
> ¼ cup Splenda Granular
> 1 cup frozen unsweetened peach slices
> ½ cup frozen unsweetened bing or sweet cherries

In a blender container, combine milk, half & half, and Splenda. Cover and process on BLEND for 10 seconds. Add peaches and cherries. Re-cover and process on BLEND for 30 to 35 seconds or until mixture is smooth. Evenly pour into 2 glasses. Serve at once.

Each serving equals:

HE: 1½ Fruit • ½ Fat-Free Milk • ¼ Slider •
2 Optional Calories

124 Calories • 0 gm Fat • 6 gm Protein •
25 gm Carbohydrate • 79 mg Sodium •
184 mg Calcium • 2 gm Fiber

DIABETIC EXCHANGES: 1½ Fruit • ½ Fat-Free Milk

Cherry Berry Smoothie

They're red, they're oh-so-sweet, and together they produce an astonishingly sumptuous smoothie! This is the rosiest of all my berry drinks, and it's a great way to celebrate a red-letter day!

◐ Serves 2 (1½ cups)

½ cup frozen unsweetened bing or dark sweet cherries
½ cup frozen unsweetened red raspberries
2 tablespoons Splenda Granular
¼ cup cold Diet Mountain Dew
1 cup cold fat-free milk or soy milk

In a blender container, combine cherries, raspberries, Splenda, and Diet Mountain Dew. Cover and process on BLEND for 20 seconds. Add milk. Re-cover and process on BLEND for 15 to 20 seconds or until mixture is smooth. Evenly pour into 2 glasses. Serve at once.

Each serving equals:

HE: 1 Fruit • ½ Fat-Free Milk • 6 Optional Calories

88 Calories • 0 gm Fat • 5 gm Protein •
17 gm Carbohydrate • 66 mg Sodium •
163 mg Calcium • 3 gm Fiber

DIABETIC EXCHANGES: 1 Fruit • ½ Fat-Free Milk

Creamy Purple Passion Smoothie

I can't promise you that this velvety, lovely beverage will increase the romance in your life—but it's certainly possible! Just be sure to serve it only to someone whose affection you're sure you want more of!   ☉   Serves 2 (1½ cups)

> 1 (8-ounce) can pear halves, packed in fruit juice, undrained
> 1 cup cold fat-free milk or soy milk
> 2 tablespoons Splenda Granular
> ¾ cup frozen unsweetened blueberries

In a blender container, combine undrained pears, milk, and Splenda. Cover and process on BLEND for 20 seconds. Add blueberries. Re-cover and process on BLEND for 20 to 25 seconds or until mixture is smooth. Evenly pour into 2 glasses. Serve at once.

Each serving equals:

HE: 1½ Fruit • ½ Fat-Free Milk • 6 Optional Calories

112 Calories • 0 gm Fat • 5 gm Protein •
23 gm Carbohydrate • 66 mg Sodium •
160 mg Calcium • 3 gm Fiber

DIABETIC EXCHANGES: 1½ Fruit • ½ Fat-Free Milk

Mint of Riches Smoothie

Hmm—a mint is where we keep our precious stuff (money), and mint is also a flavor so rich it belongs only in our most fabulous desserts and drinks. Sounds like they are parts of the same great idea: only the best! This is a creamy, fruity, cooler-than-cool treat!

◐ Serves 2 (1¼ cups)

> 1 (8-ounce) can pear halves, packed in fruit juice, undrained
> 1 cup cold fat-free milk or soy milk
> 2 tablespoons Splenda Granular
> ⅛ teaspoon mint extract
> ¾ cup frozen unsweetened red raspberries

In a blender container, combine undrained pears, milk, Splenda, and mint extract. Cover and process on BLEND for 15 seconds. Add raspberries. Re-cover and process on BLEND for 15 to 20 seconds or until mixture is smooth. Evenly pour into 2 glasses. Serve at once.

Each serving equals:

HE: 1½ Fruit • ½ Fat-Free Milk • 6 Optional Calories

104 Calories • 0 gm Fat • 5 gm Protein •
21 gm Carbohydrate • 66 mg Sodium •
165 mg Calcium • 5 gm Fiber

DIABETIC EXCHANGES: 1½ Fruit • ½ Fat-Free Milk

Chocolate Almond Smoothie

If you've ever lusted for the most luxurious chocolate almond ice cream, here's the good news: You can leave that high-fat pint in the store freezer and instead fulfill all your chocolate almond fantasies with this spectacular smoothie!   ☻   Serves 2 (2 cups)

1½ cups cold fat-free milk or soy milk

2 tablespoons Hershey's Lite Chocolate Syrup

2 tablespoons Splenda Granular

½ teaspoon almond extract

1½ cups crushed ice

2 tablespoons Cool Whip Lite

2 teaspoons slivered almonds

In a blender container, combine milk, chocolate syrup, Splenda, and almond extract. Cover and process on BLEND for 10 seconds. Add ice. Re-cover and process on BLEND for 15 to 20 seconds or until mixture is smooth. Evenly pour into 2 glasses. Top each glass with 1 tablespoon Cool Whip Lite and 1 teaspoon almonds. Serve at once.

Each serving equals:

HE: ¾ Fat-Free Milk • ½ Slider • 8 Optional Calories

---

120 Calories • 2 gm Fat • 9 gm Protein •
17 gm Carbohydrate • 152 mg Sodium •
233 mg Calcium • 0 gm Fiber

DIABETIC EXCHANGES: 1 Fat-Free Milk •
½ Starch/Carbohydrate

Go for It

Cultured Classics

Yogurt delivers so much healthy nutrition, it's an ideal addition to a smoothie. As long as you've got a container of fat-free yogurt on hand, you're ready to roll with some spectacular combinations. On those days when you're rushing to class or to a kids' after-school sporting event, a yogurt smoothie is a handy meal-on-the-run.

Starting today, stock your house with the fixings for all your favorites, and you'll never have to stop for fast food en route again!

Go for It Cultured Classics

Banana and Peach Smoothie

I'm starting this section with a smoothie classic—a few perfect peaches, one beautiful banana, and just enough yogurt to deliver a dream of a drink! Remember, *really* ripe bananas taste best in smoothies.   ☉   Serves 2 (1 cup)

> 1 (8-ounce) can sliced peaches, packed in fruit juice, undrained
> 1 cup (1 medium) diced banana
> ¼ cup Splenda Granular
> ¾ cup Dannon plain fat-free yogurt

In a blender container, combine undrained peaches, banana, and Splenda. Cover and process on BLEND for 15 seconds. Add yogurt. Re-cover and process on BLEND for 15 to 20 seconds or until mixture is smooth. Evenly pour into 2 glasses. Serve at once.

Each serving equals:

HE: 2 Fruit • ½ Fat-Free Milk • 6 Optional Calories

176 Calories • 0 gm Fat • 6 gm Protein •
38 gm Carbohydrate • 69 mg Sodium •
117 mg Calcium • 3 gm Fiber

DIABETIC EXCHANGES: 2 Fruit • ½ Fat-Free Milk

Cherry Pineapple Smoothie

Pineapple arrives with so much of its own natural sweetness, you need to add very little additional sweetener. Same with cherries, depending on whether the crop was as delectably ripe as can be when it was picked and flash frozen. Sweets for the sweet!

❂ Serves 2 (1¼ cups)

> 1 (8-ounce) can crushed pineapple, packed in fruit juice, undrained
> 1 cup frozen unsweetened bing or sweet cherries
> 2 tablespoons Splenda Granular
> ¾ cup Dannon plain fat-free yogurt

In a blender container, combine undrained pineapple, cherries, and Splenda. Cover and process on BLEND for 30 seconds. Add yogurt. Re-cover and process on BLEND for 15 to 20 seconds or until mixture is smooth. Evenly pour into 2 glasses. Serve at once.

Each serving equals:

HE: 2 Fruit • ½ Fat-Free Milk • 6 Optional Calories

---

144 Calories • 0 gm Fat • 6 gm Protein •
30 gm Carbohydrate • 72 mg Sodium •
211 mg Calcium • 2 gm Fiber

DIABETIC EXCHANGES: 2 Fruit • ½ Fat-Free Milk

Very Berry Smoothie

Why do I suggest cold Diet Mountain Dew in my smoothie recipes, you may wonder? Warm soda tends to get foamy when blended and doesn't taste nearly as good. This combo is, in the words of my grandkids, "berry berry delicious!"   ☻   Serves 2 (1 cup)

> ½ cup cold Diet Mountain Dew
> ¾ cup frozen unsweetened blueberries
> ¾ cup frozen unsweetened red raspberries
> ¾ cup Dannon plain fat-free yogurt
> ¼ cup Splenda Granular

In a blender container, combine Diet Mountain Dew, blueberries, and raspberries. Cover and process on BLEND for 15 seconds. Add yogurt and Splenda. Re-cover and process on BLEND for 15 to 20 seconds or until mixture is smooth. Evenly pour into 2 glasses. Serve at once.

Each serving equals:

HE: 1 Fruit • ½ Fat-Free Milk • 6 Optional Calories

---

108 Calories • 0 gm Fat • 6 gm Protein •
21 gm Carbohydrate • 77 mg Sodium •
197 mg Calcium • 4 gm Fiber

DIABETIC EXCHANGES: 1 Fruit • ½ Fat-Free Milk

Creamy Peach Melba Smoothie

If ever a smoothie might make you want to sing for your supper, this might be the one! Raspberry and peach are a nearly perfect couple, don't you agree? Share this with your sweetheart and see what develops! ☻ Serves 2 (1 cup)

1 (8-ounce) can sliced peaches, packed in fruit juice, undrained
¾ cup frozen unsweetened red raspberries
¼ cup Splenda Granular
¾ cup Dannon plain fat-free yogurt

In a blender container, combine undrained peaches, raspberries, and Splenda. Cover and process on BLEND for 30 seconds. Add yogurt. Re-cover and process on BLEND for 15 to 20 seconds or until mixture is smooth. Evenly pour into 2 glasses. Serve at once.

Each serving equals:

HE: 1½ Fruit • ½ Fat-Free Milk • 12 Optional Calories

152 Calories • 0 gm Fat • 6 gm Protein •
32 gm Carbohydrate • 89 mg Sodium •
193 mg Calcium • 4 gm Fiber

DIABETIC EXCHANGES: 1½ Fruit • ½ Fat-Free Milk

Razzle-Dazzle Raspberry Smoothie

The great Broadway musical and movie of *Chicago* features a sizzling number about giving the customers "the old razzle-dazzle," a breathtaking, heartstopping dance number that ends in a standing ovation. Well, I can't promise your family will stand up and cheer after a gulp of this—but they might!

◐ Serves 2 (1¼ cups)

> 1 (8-ounce) can crushed pineapple, packed in fruit juice,
>   undrained
> ¼ cup cold Diet Mountain Dew
> ¾ cup frozen unsweetened red raspberries
> ¾ cup Dannon plain fat-free yogurt

In a blender container, combine undrained pineapple, Diet Mountain Dew, and raspberries. Cover and process on BLEND for 20 seconds. Add yogurt. Re-cover and process on BLEND for 15 to 20 seconds or until mixture is smooth. Evenly pour into 2 glasses. Serve at once.

Each serving equals:

HE: 1½ Fruit • ½ Fat-Free Milk

112 Calories • 0 gm Fat • 6 gm Protein •
22 gm Carbohydrate • 75 mg Sodium •
210 mg Calcium • 4 gm Fiber

DIABETIC EXCHANGES: 1½ Fruit • ½ Fat-Free Milk

Raspberry Sunrise Smoothie

I'm a very early riser, so I've seen more than my share of magnificent sunrises, when I feel that each new day is a kind of miracle. I created this smoothie in the glorious colors of dawn, but that doesn't mean you can't enjoy it anytime you wish. Go for it!

◐ Serves 2 (1 cup)

> ½ cup cold unsweetened orange juice
> ¾ cup Dannon plain fat-free yogurt
> ¼ cup Splenda Granular
> 1½ cups frozen unsweetened red raspberries

In a blender container, combine orange juice, yogurt, and Splenda. Cover and process on BLEND for 10 seconds. Add raspberries. Re-cover and process on BLEND for 20 to 25 seconds or until mixture is smooth. Evenly pour into 2 glasses. Serve at once.

Each serving equals:

HE: 1½ Fruit • ½ Fat-Free Milk • 6 Optional Calories

---

128 Calories • 0 gm Fat • 6 gm Protein •
26 gm Carbohydrate • 72 mg Sodium •
208 mg Calcium • 6 gm Fiber

DIABETIC EXCHANGES: 1½ Fruit • ½ Fat-Free Milk

Orange Crush Smoothie

The exquisite essence of orange, that fruit containing all the light of the sun, brings its unique intensity to this blender delight. Orange juice has always contained the juices of a mélange of different oranges, and all that splendid flavor is downright irresistible!

❂ Serves 2 (1½ cups)

> 1 (8-ounce) can crushed pineapple, packed in fruit juice,
>   undrained
> 1 cup cold unsweetened orange juice
> 2 tablespoons Splenda Granular
> ¾ cup Dannon plain fat-free yogurt

In a blender container, combine undrained pineapple, orange juice, and Splenda. Cover and process on BLEND for 20 seconds. Add yogurt. Re-cover and process on BLEND for 30 to 35 seconds or until mixture is smooth. Evenly pour into 2 glasses. Serve at once.

Each serving equals:

HE: 2 Fruit • ½ Fat-Free Milk • 6 Optional Calories

144 Calories • 0 gm Fat • 6 gm Protein • 30 gm Carbohydrate • 74 mg Sodium • 210 mg Calcium • 1 gm Fiber

DIABETIC EXCHANGES: 2 Fruit • ½ Fat-Free Milk

Creamy Tropical Isle Fruit Smoothie

You might want to think about drinking this tasty party-in-a-glass from one of those hollowed-out coconut shells—it's that convincing that you're reclining on a chaise under a Caribbean sky! You'll be astonished how much flavor just a bit of spreadable fruit can add!

● Serves 2 (1¼ cups)

> ½ cup cold unsweetened orange juice
> 1 (8-ounce) can crushed pineapple, packed in fruit juice,
>   undrained
> 1 tablespoon apricot spreadable fruit
> ¼ cup Splenda Granular
> ¾ cup Dannon plain fat-free yogurt

In a blender container, combine orange juice, undrained pineapple, spreadable fruit, and Splenda. Cover and process on BLEND for 20 seconds. Add yogurt. Re-cover and process on BLEND for 15 to 20 seconds or until mixture is smooth. Evenly pour into 2 glasses. Serve at once.

Each serving equals:

HE: 2 Fruit • ½ Fat-Free Milk • 12 Optional Calories

---

168 Calories • 0 gm Fat • 6 gm Protein • 36 gm Carbohydrate • 73 mg Sodium • 207 mg Calcium • 2 gm Fiber

---

DIABETIC EXCHANGES: 2 Fruit • ½ Fat-Free Milk

Ambrosia Smoothie

Food of the gods, the ancient peoples called ambrosia, but in modern times, we use the word to describe something almost too good for this world! Do you deserve a beverage so spectacularly delectable you'll think you've gone to heaven after just one sip? Of course you do!   ◐   Serves 2 (1 cup)

1 (8-ounce) can crushed pineapple, packed in fruit juice,
     undrained
1 cup (1 medium) diced banana
¼ cup Splenda Granular
½ teaspoon coconut extract
¾ cup Dannon plain fat-free yogurt

In a blender container, combine undrained pineapple, banana, Splenda, and coconut extract. Cover and process on BLEND for 20 seconds. Add yogurt. Re-cover and process on BLEND for 15 to 20 seconds or until mixture is smooth. Evenly pour into 2 glasses. Serve at once.

Each serving equals:

HE: 2 Fruit • ½ Fat-Free Milk • 12 Optional Calories

168 Calories • 0 gm Fat • 6 gm Protein •
36 gm Carbohydrate • 72 mg Sodium •
204 mg Calcium • 3 gm Fiber

DIABETIC EXCHANGES: 2 Fruit • ½ Fat-Free Milk

Heavenly Kiwi Pineapple Smoothie

I've never been to New Zealand, but when I first saw and then tasted the odd little egg-shaped kiwifruits, I decided it must be an extraordinary place! How else could it have given us a treat that tastes of strawberry and banana and—well, something else I just can't describe. You'll have to try it yourself!

◑ Serves 2 (1½ cups)

> 1 (8-ounce) can crushed pineapple, packed in fruit juice, undrained
> 2 kiwifruit, peeled and diced
> ½ cup cold Diet Mountain Dew
> ¾ cup Dannon plain fat-free yogurt
> ¼ cup Splenda Granular

In a blender container, combine undrained pineapple, kiwi, and Diet Mountain Dew. Cover and process on BLEND for 15 seconds. Add yogurt and Splenda. Re-cover and process on BLEND for 15 to 20 seconds or until mixture is smooth. Evenly pour into 2 glasses. Serve at once.

Each serving equals:

HE: 2 Fruit • ½ Fat-Free Milk • 6 Optional Calories

152 Calories • 0 gm Fat • 7 gm Protein •
31 gm Carbohydrate • 78 mg Sodium •
230 mg Calcium • 3 gm Fiber

DIABETIC EXCHANGES: 2 Fruit • ½ Fat-Free Milk

Peach and Pineapple Fling Smoothie

To me, a fling always meant doing something a bit outrageous and following your heart, which might be why I named this smoothie as I did. On one of those days when you're about to launch a new business, go on a fix-up date, or just redecorate your bedroom, throw caution to the wind and drink this!

◐ Serves 2 (1¼ cups)

> 1 (8-ounce) can crushed pineapple, packed in fruit juice, undrained
> ¼ cup cold Diet Mountain Dew
> 2 tablespoons Splenda Granular
> 1 cup frozen unsweetened sliced peaches
> ¾ cup Dannon plain fat-free yogurt

In a blender container, combine undrained pineapple, Diet Mountain Dew, Splenda, and peaches. Cover and process on BLEND for 30 seconds. Add yogurt. Re-cover and process on BLEND for 20 to 25 seconds or until mixture is smooth. Evenly pour into 2 glasses. Serve at once.

Each serving equals:

HE: 2 Fruit • ½ Fat-Free Milk • 6 Optional Calories

132 Calories • 0 gm Fat • 6 gm Protein •
27 gm Carbohydrate • 75 mg Sodium •
204 mg Calcium • 2 gm Fiber

DIABETIC EXCHANGES: 2 Fruit • ½ Fat-Free Milk

Heavenly Hawaiian Smoothie

You'll find bananas in so many smoothie recipes because they act as a natural thickener and provide a truly luscious texture. You may want to experiment with freezing your bananas in slices and then dicing just before using them. ☾   Serves 2 (1¼ cups)

1 (8-ounce) can crushed pineapple, packed in fruit juice,
*   undrained*
1 cup (1 medium) diced banana
¼ cup cold Diet Mountain Dew
¾ cup Dannon plain fat-free yogurt

In a blender container, combine undrained pineapple, banana, and Diet Mountain Dew. Cover and process on BLEND for 15 seconds. Add yogurt. Re-cover and process on BLEND for 15 to 20 seconds or until mixture is smooth. Evenly pour into 2 glasses. Serve at once.

Each serving equals:

HE: 2 Fruit • ½ Fat-Free Milk

160 Calories • 0 gm Fat • 6 gm Protein •
34 gm Carbohydrate • 75 mg Sodium •
204 mg Calcium • 3 gm Fiber

DIABETIC EXCHANGES: 2 Fruit • ½ Fat-Free Milk

Pear and Coconut Cream Smoothie

Talk about temptation! Pears are a kind of luxury fruit when you buy them fresh—not especially expensive, but somehow a bit more special than your everyday apples and oranges. The canned variety are one of my favorite childhood desserts, and even now, I love their cool, smooth texture. Combined with two kinds of coconut flavor, they take on a party appeal that my daughter-in-law Angie will adore! ☻ Serves 2 (1 cup)

> 1 (8-ounce) can pear halves, packed in fruit juice, undrained
> 1 cup (1 medium) diced banana
> 2 tablespoons cold Diet Mountain Dew
> 2 tablespoons Splenda Granular
> 1/2 teaspoon coconut extract
> 3/4 cup Dannon plain fat-free yogurt
> 2 teaspoons flaked coconut

In a blender container, combine undrained pears, banana, Diet Mountain Dew, Splenda, and coconut extract. Cover and process on BLEND for 20 seconds. Add yogurt and coconut. Re-cover and process on BLEND for 15 to 20 seconds or until mixture is smooth. Evenly pour into 2 glasses. Serve at once.

Each serving equals:

HE: 2 Fruit • 1/2 Fat-Free Milk • 1/4 Slider • 1 Optional Calorie

164 Calories • 1 gm Fat • 6 gm Protein • 35 gm Carbohydrate • 79 mg Sodium • 192 mg Calcium • 3 gm Fiber

DIABETIC EXCHANGES: 2 Fruit • 1/2 Fat-Free Milk

Strawberries Romanoff Smoothie

The Romanovs (also sometimes spelled with "ff") were a Russian ruling family for whom nothing was too rich, too sweet, or too much trouble! Jewelers created fantastic gems, architects designed amazing palaces, and chefs worked night and day to please them. At the heart of the fancy restaurant dessert called Strawberries Romanoff is the pleasurable partnership between strawberry and orange flavors, and here they shine as brightly!

◑ Serves 2 (1¼ cups)

> ½ cup cold unsweetened orange juice
> ¾ cup Dannon plain fat-free yogurt
> ¼ cup Splenda Granular
> 2 cups frozen unsweetened strawberries

In a blender container, combine orange juice, yogurt, and Splenda. Cover and process on BLEND for 10 seconds. Add strawberries. Re-cover and process on BLEND for 20 to 25 seconds or until mixture is smooth. Evenly pour into 2 glasses. Serve at once.

Each serving equals:

HE: 1½ Fruit • ½ Fat-Free Milk • 12 Optional Calories

168 Calories • 0 gm Fat • 6 gm Protein •
36 gm Carbohydrate • 76 mg Sodium •
223 mg Calcium • 4 gm Fiber

DIABETIC EXCHANGES: 1½ Fruit • ½ Fat-Free Milk

Fuzzy Navel Smoothie

When I first heard this name for a bar drink that starred peaches and cream, I thought that it sounded a little bit strange. (After all, who *wants* a real-life fuzzy navel?) But the sumptuous combination of flavors is too good to resist. Let's get fuzzy!

◑ Serves 2 (1 cup)

> ½ cup cold unsweetened orange juice
> 1 (8-ounce) can sliced peaches, packed in fruit juice, undrained
> 2 tablespoons Splenda Granular
> ¼ teaspoon vanilla extract
> ¾ cup Dannon plain fat-free yogurt

In a blender container, combine orange juice, undrained peaches, Splenda, and vanilla extract. Cover and process on BLEND for 15 seconds. Add yogurt. Re-cover and process on BLEND for 15 to 20 seconds or until mixture is smooth. Evenly pour into 2 glasses. Serve at once.

Each serving equals:

HE: 1½ Fruit • ½ Fat-Free Milk • 6 Optional Calories

148 Calories • 0 gm Fat • 5 gm Protein •
32 gm Carbohydrate • 90 mg Sodium •
188 mg Calcium • 1 gm Fiber

DIABETIC EXCHANGES: 1½ Fruit • ½ Fat-Free Milk

Mango Creamsicle Smoothie

Are creamsicles one of the tastes of childhood that you've never forgotten? Good, then there are lots of us out there! Here's my version of a frozen dessert specialty reinvented for the adult palate, with the succulent flavor of mangos added to that creamy orange dream!

● Serves 2 (1 cup)

> ½ cup cold unsweetened orange juice
> 1 cup (2 medium) sliced fresh ripe mango
> 2 tablespoons Splenda Granular
> ¾ cup Dannon plain fat-free yogurt

In a blender container, combine orange juice, mango, and Splenda. Cover and process on BLEND for 20 seconds. Add yogurt. Re-cover and process on BLEND for 15 to 20 seconds or until mixture is smooth. Evenly pour into 2 glasses. Serve at once.

HINT: 1 cup sliced canned mango, drained, may be used in place of fresh mango.

Each serving equals:

HE: 1½ Fruit • ½ Fat-Free Milk • 6 Optional Calories

140 Calories • 0 gm Fat • 6 gm Protein •
29 gm Carbohydrate • 74 mg Sodium •
196 mg Calcium • 1 gm Fiber

DIABETIC EXCHANGES: 1½ Fruit • ½ Fat-Free Milk

Cranberry Passion Smoothie

When I get excited about something, it's true—my cheeks do get rosy and my eyes shine extra bright. If you want to get that feeling and that certain glow, here's the smoothie that can do it! Isn't love grand?   ☻   Serves 2 (1¼ cups)

> 1 cup cold Ocean Spray reduced-calorie cranberry juice cocktail
> ¾ cup frozen unsweetened blueberries
> ¼ cup Splenda Granular
> 1½ cups Dannon plain fat-free yogurt

In a blender container, combine cranberry juice cocktail, blueberries, and Splenda. Cover and process on BLEND for 30 seconds. Add yogurt. Re-cover and process on BLEND for 15 to 20 seconds or until mixture is smooth. Evenly pour into 2 glasses. Serve at once.

Each serving equals:

HE: 1 Fat-Free Milk • 1 Fruit • 12 Optional Calories

---

156 Calories • 0 gm Fat • 10 gm Protein •
29 gm Carbohydrate • 146 mg Sodium •
381 mg Calcium • 1 gm Fiber

DIABETIC EXCHANGES: 1 Fat-Free Milk • 1 Fruit

Vineyard Smoothie

There's a truly scrumptious intensity to a multilayered berry beverage like this one. Orchard and vineyard fruits pack so much enticing flavor into each tiny berry and grape. No need to go wine-tasting when you can relax at home with a glass of this!

◑ Serves 2 (1 cup)

> ½ cup cold unsweetened grape juice
> ¾ cup frozen unsweetened red raspberries
> ¾ cup frozen unsweetened blueberries
> 2 tablespoons Splenda Granular
> ¾ cup Dannon plain fat-free yogurt

In a blender container, combine grape juice, raspberries, blueberries, and Splenda. Cover and process on BLEND for 30 seconds. Add yogurt. Re-cover and process on BLEND for 15 to 20 seconds or until mixture is smooth. Evenly pour into 2 glasses. Serve at once.

Each serving equals:

HE: 1½ Fruit • ½ Fat-Free Milk • 6 Optional Calories

144 Calories • 0 gm Fat • 6 gm Protein •
30 gm Carbohydrate • 73 mg Sodium •
203 mg Calcium • 5 gm Fiber

DIABETIC EXCHANGES: 1½ Fruit • ½ Fat-Free Milk

Banana Coconut Cream Smoothie

With double the dairy and double the coconut, this velvety concoction is as lipsmacking good as it is good for you! Instead of losing your head over a couple of slices of coconut cream pie, why not revel in a tall glass of this—and then dance the night away!

◐ Serves 2 (1¼ cups)

1 cup cold fat-free milk or soy milk
1 cup (1 medium) diced banana
1 teaspoon coconut extract
¾ cup Dannon plain fat-free yogurt
2 tablespoons Splenda Granular
2 tablespoons flaked coconut

In a blender container, combine milk, banana, and coconut extract. Cover and process on BLEND for 15 seconds. Add yogurt, Splenda, and coconut. Re-cover and process on BLEND for 15 to 20 seconds or until mixture is smooth. Evenly pour into 2 glasses. Serve at once.

Each serving equals:

HE: 1 Fat-Free Milk • 1 Fruit • ¼ Slider •
1 Optional Calorie

194 Calories • 2 gm Fat • 10 gm Protein •
34 gm Carbohydrate • 147 mg Sodium •
338 mg Calcium • 2 gm Fiber

DIABETIC EXCHANGES: 1 Fat-Free Milk • 1 Fruit •
½ Fat

Cookies & Cream Banana Smoothie

I wonder who invented the luscious flavor that combined chocolate cookies and creamy vanilla ice cream. (He or she is a hero to millions!) Now you can revisit those glory days in a yogurt shake that is as rich as it is fun to drink! My daughter-in-law Pam loves creamy drinks like this one. ☻ Serves 2 (1 cup)

1½ cups Dannon plain fat-free yogurt
1 cup (1 medium) sliced banana
½ teaspoon vanilla extract
2 tablespoons Splenda Granular
2 SnackWell's chocolate sandwich cookies, broken into large pieces

In a blender container, combine yogurt, banana, vanilla extract, and Splenda. Cover and process on BLEND for 30 seconds. Add cookie pieces. Re-cover and process on BLEND for 25 to 30 seconds. Evenly pour into 2 glasses. Serve at once.

Each serving equals:

HE: 1 Fat-Free Milk • 1 Fruit • ¾ Slider

226 Calories • 2 gm Fat • 12 gm Protein •
40 gm Carbohydrate • 190 mg Sodium •
379 mg Calcium • 2 gm Fiber

DIABETIC EXCHANGES: 1 Fat-Free Milk • 1 Fruit •
1 Starch

Banana Maple Smoothie

If you're hungry for pancakes with syrup but haven't got the time, why not substitute this delectable blend of bananas, yogurt, and the tastiest "lite" syrup I've ever found? It's downright yummy, and kids love it, too!   ☾   Serves 2 (1¼ cups)

> 1 cup (1 medium) sliced banana
> 2 tablespoons Log Cabin Sugar Free Maple Syrup
> 1½ cups Dannon plain fat-free yogurt
> 2 tablespoons Splenda Granular
> ¼ teaspoon vanilla extract

In a blender container, combine banana, maple syrup, yogurt, Splenda, and vanilla extract. Cover and process on BLEND for 20 to 25 seconds or until mixture is smooth. Evenly pour into 2 glasses. Serve at once.

Each serving equals:

HE: 1 Fat-Free Milk • 1 Fruit • 16 Optional Calories

---

184 Calories • 0 gm Fat • 11 gm Protein •
35 gm Carbohydrate • 142 mg Sodium •
370 mg Calcium • 2 gm Fiber

DIABETIC EXCHANGES: 1 Fat-Free Milk • 1 Fruit

Peachy Lime Smoothie

When I'm recipe testing and creating, I like to think of myself as a kitchen scientist, a culinary chemist stirring up eat-and-drink experiments to surprise and satisfy my readers. I've always liked the tart taste of lime but had not yet used it much in my smoothie recipes. Here's one where I think it works brilliantly!

● Serves 2 (1¼ cups)

¾ cup Dannon plain fat-free yogurt
½ cup cold Diet Mountain Dew
¼ cup Splenda Granular
2 teaspoons lime juice
1½ cups frozen unsweetened sliced peaches

In a blender container, combine yogurt, Diet Mountain Dew, Splenda, and lime juice. Cover and process on BLEND for 15 seconds. Add peaches. Re-cover and process on BLEND for 20 to 25 seconds or until mixture is smooth. Evenly pour into 2 glasses. Serve at once.

Each serving equals:

HE: 1½ Fruit • ½ Fat-Free Milk • 12 Optional Calories

124 Calories • 0 gm Fat • 6 gm Protein •
25 gm Carbohydrate • 77 mg Sodium •
190 mg Calcium • 2 gm Fiber

DIABETIC EXCHANGES: 1½ Fruit • ½ Fat-Free Milk

Amaretto Peach Smoothie

Just because you've chosen to enjoy a non-alcoholic lifestyle (and many of us have) doesn't mean you must miss out on some of those bar-style creamy drinks. This sumptuous combination uses just a drop of almond flavor to add a glorious gloss to a great peach drink.

● Serves 2 (1 cup)

> 1 (8-ounce) can sliced peaches, packed in fruit juice, undrained
> ¼ cup cold fat-free milk or soy milk
> ¼ cup Splenda Granular
> ½ teaspoon almond extract
> ¾ cup Dannon plain fat-free yogurt

In a blender container, combine undrained peaches, milk, Splenda, and almond extract. Cover and process on BLEND for 30 seconds. Add yogurt. Re-cover and process on BLEND for 15 to 20 seconds or until mixture is smooth. Evenly pour into 2 glasses. Serve at once.

Each serving equals:

HE: 1 Fruit • ½ Fat-Free Milk • ¼ Slider • 2 Optional Calories

---

136 Calories • 0 gm Fat • 6 gm Protein • 28 gm Carbohydrate • 104 mg Sodium • 220 mg Calcium • 1 gm Fiber

---

DIABETIC EXCHANGES: 1 Fruit • ½ Fat-Free Milk

Creamy Apricot Smoothie

To me, apricots are little golden gems of sweetness, perfect for party desserts and drinks where you want to hear a few "oohs" and "aahs." But don't save this only for times when you have a houseful of guests. Treat yourself like company and enjoy!

○ Serves 2 (1 cup)

> 1 (8-ounce) can apricot halves, packed in fruit juice, undrained
> ¼ cup Splenda Granular
> 1½ cups Dannon plain fat-free yogurt

In a blender container, combine undrained apricots and Splenda. Cover and process on BLEND for 15 seconds. Add yogurt. Re-cover and process on BLEND for 15 to 20 seconds or until mixture is smooth. Evenly pour into 2 glasses. Serve at once.

Each serving equals:

HE: 1 Fat-Free Milk • 1 Fruit • 12 Optional Calories

168 Calories • 0 gm Fat • 11 gm Protein •
31 gm Carbohydrate • 146 mg Sodium •
379 mg Calcium • 2 gm Fiber

DIABETIC EXCHANGES: 1 Fat-Free Milk • 1 Fruit

Double Apricot Smoothie

Layers of flavor is one of a successful cook's repertoire of kitchen "tricks" and one that I use often. Here, the combination of two forms of delightfully alluring apricots makes this beautifully colored smoothie a winner! ◐ Serves 2 (1¼ cups)

1 (8-ounce) can apricots, packed in fruit juice, undrained
2 tablespoons apricot spreadable fruit
2 tablespoons Splenda Granular
½ cup crushed ice
¾ cup Dannon plain fat-free yogurt

In a blender container, combine undrained apricots, spreadable fruit, Splenda, and ice. Cover and process on BLEND for 30 seconds. Add yogurt. Re-cover and process on BLEND for 10 to 15 seconds or until mixture is smooth. Evenly pour into 2 glasses. Serve at once.

Each serving equals:

HE: 2 Fruit • ½ Fat-Free Milk • 6 Optional Calories

148 Calories • 0 gm Fat • 6 gm Protein •
31 gm Carbohydrate • 75 mg Sodium •
196 mg Calcium • 2 gm Fiber

DIABETIC EXCHANGES: 2 Fruit • ½ Fat-Free Milk

Strawberry Yogurt Smoothie

I've probably made more strawberry smoothies than any other kinds, simply because I personally love that rosy gem best. You'll find plenty of my favorites in this book, but this is one I think delivers some of the sweetest and best flavor. Almond and strawberry may seem to you like an unusual pairing, but it works!

◐ Serves 2 (1 full cup)

¾ cup Dannon plain fat-free yogurt
¼ cup Splenda Granular
½ teaspoon almond extract
⅓ cup cold fat-free milk or soy milk
1½ cups frozen unsweetened strawberries

In a blender container, combine yogurt, Splenda, almond extract, and milk. Cover and process on BLEND for 15 seconds. Add strawberries. Re-cover and process on BLEND for 25 to 30 seconds or until mixture is smooth. Evenly pour into 2 glasses. Serve at once.

Each serving equals:

HE: ¾ Fruit • ½ Fat-Free Milk • ¼ Slider •
7 Optional Calories

124 Calories • 0 gm Fat • 6 gm Protein •
25 gm Carbohydrate • 93 mg Sodium •
256 mg Calcium • 3 gm Fiber

DIABETIC EXCHANGES: 1 Fruit • ½ Fat-Free Milk

Raspberry Joy Smoothie

When fresh, they are delicate and easily bruised, but often impossibly sweet and utterly delicious. Raspberries produce a wonderfully satisfying smoothie, on their own and in partnership with other intense flavors like the coconut here. As the saying goes: Choose to be happy. Choose joy!   ☉   Serves 2 (1 cup)

¾ cup Dannon plain fat-free yogurt
½ cup cold Diet Mountain Dew
¼ cup Splenda Granular
½ teaspoon coconut extract
1½ cups frozen unsweetened red raspberries

In a blender container, combine yogurt, Diet Mountain Dew, Splenda, and coconut extract. Cover and process on BLEND for 15 seconds. Add raspberries. Re-cover and process on BLEND for 25 to 30 seconds or until mixture is smooth. Evenly pour into 2 glasses. Serve at once.

Each serving equals:

HE: 1 Fruit • ½ Fat-Free Milk • 6 Optional Calories

104 Calories • 0 gm Fat • 6 gm Protein •
20 gm Carbohydrate • 73 mg Sodium •
203 mg Calcium • 6 gm Fiber

DIABETIC EXCHANGES: 1 Fruit • ½ Fat-Free Milk

Vanilla Blueberry Smoothie

They are naturally sweet and tart all at once, and they turn whatever they're blended with a luscious shade of pale purple. Blueberries are one of my favorite tiny temptations—and they freeze beautifully, which makes them a natural for smoothies.

❤ Serves 2 (1½ cups)

> 1½ cups Dannon plain fat-free yogurt
> 2 tablespoons Splenda Granular
> 2 tablespoons cold Diet Mountain Dew
> 1 teaspoon vanilla extract
> 1½ cups frozen unsweetened blueberries

In a blender container, combine yogurt, Splenda, Diet Mountain Dew, and vanilla extract. Cover and process on BLEND for 10 seconds. Add blueberries. Re-cover and process on BLEND for 15 to 20 seconds or until mixture is smooth. Evenly pour into 2 glasses. Serve at once.

Each serving equals:

HE: 1 Fat-Free Milk • 1 Fruit • 6 Optional Calories

173 Calories • 1 gm Fat • 11 gm Protein •
30 gm Carbohydrate • 144 mg Sodium •
375 mg Calcium • 3 gm Fiber

DIABETIC EXCHANGES: 1 Fat-Free Milk • 1 Fruit

Cherry Cream Smoothie

If you're having trouble finding some frozen fruits in your grocer's freezer, speak up! This is the age of the smoothie and believe me, if you're eager to purchase frozen cherries but can't find them, you're not alone—even if, like me, you live in a pretty small town. Ask your store to carry as many different frozen fruits as they've got room for. They're a healthy alternative and a vital part of a living-well diet for all ages!   ☯   Serves 2 (1½ cups)

½ cup cold Diet Mountain Dew
1 cup frozen unsweetened tart red cherries
1½ cups Dannon plain fat-free yogurt
¼ cup Splenda Granular
½ teaspoon vanilla extract

In a blender container, combine Diet Mountain Dew and cherries. Cover and process on BLEND for 20 seconds. Add yogurt, Splenda, and vanilla extract. Re-cover and process on BLEND for 15 to 20 seconds or until mixture is smooth. Evenly pour into 2 glasses. Serve at once.

Each serving equals:

HE: 1 Fat-Free Milk • 1 Fruit • 12 Optional Calories

148 Calories • 0 gm Fat • 11 gm Protein •
26 gm Carbohydrate • 150 mg Sodium •
378 mg Calcium • 1 gm Fiber

DIABETIC EXCHANGES: 1 Fat-Free Milk • 1 Fruit

Kiwi Lemon Cream Smoothie

You didn't think that I'd write an entire book of recipes without some JELL-O, did you? Here's a wonderful way to incorporate the delightful sweet-tart taste of lemon without worrying about keeping fresh lemons on hand through the winter, when you really need a burst of sunshine on gloomy days. Make sure you peel your kiwifruit well; its skin is too tough to "blend" away.

☻ Serves 2 (1¼ cups)

> ½ cup cold Diet Mountain Dew
> 1 (4-serving) package JELL-O sugar-free lemon gelatin
> ¼ cup Splenda Granular
> 1½ cups Dannon plain fat-free yogurt
> 2 kiwifruit, peeled and diced

In a blender container, combine Diet Mountain Dew, dry gelatin, and Splenda. Cover and process on BLEND for 15 seconds. Add yogurt and kiwifruit. Re-cover and process on BLEND for 15 to 20 seconds or until mixture is smooth. Evenly pour into 2 glasses. Serve at once.

Each serving equals:

HE: 1 Fat-Free Milk • 1 Fruit • 10 Optional Calories

152 Calories • 0 gm Fat • 12 gm Protein • 26 gm Carbohydrate • 157 mg Sodium • 396 mg Calcium • 2 gm Fiber

DIABETIC EXCHANGES: 1 Fat-Free Milk • 1 Fruit

Orange Buttermilk Smoothie

Are you one of those people who's always thought buttermilk was a high-fat milk that could never be part of a healthy food plan? A lot of people have the wrong idea about buttermilk, which is good for you and produces a uniquely delicious dairy shake, especially when combined with some intense fruit juice concentrate. Yum!

○ Serves 4 (1 cup)

> 1 cup cold fat-free buttermilk
> 1 (6-ounce) can frozen orange juice concentrate, partially thawed
> 1½ cups Dannon plain fat-free yogurt
> ½ cup Splenda Granular
> 1 cup crushed ice

In a blender container, combine buttermilk, orange juice concentrate, yogurt, and Splenda. Cover and process on BLEND for 20 seconds. Add ice. Re-cover and process on BLEND for 25 to 30 seconds or until mixture is smooth. Evenly pour into 4 glasses. Serve at once.

Each serving equals:

HE: 1 Fruit • ¾ Fat-Free Milk • 12 Optional Calories

104 Calories • 0 gm Fat • 8 gm Protein •
18 gm Carbohydrate • 135 mg Sodium •
258 mg Calcium • 0 gm Fiber

DIABETIC EXCHANGES: 1 Fruit • ½ Fat-Free Milk

Orange Ale Smoothie

Adding fizz to your blender container is a little like making a healthy ice cream soda! Here, the marriage between OJ and ginger ale is definitely not a one-time-only, but instead an easy and satisfying quick fix for anyone feeling less energetic than they'd like to be!

○ Serves 2 (1¼ cups)

1 cup cold unsweetened orange juice
½ cup cold diet ginger ale
¼ cup Splenda Granular
1½ cups Dannon plain fat-free yogurt

In a blender container, combine orange juice, diet ginger ale, Splenda, and yogurt. Cover and process on BLEND for 15 to 20 seconds or until mixture is smooth. Evenly pour into 2 glasses. Serve at once.

Each serving equals:

HE: 1 Fat-Free Milk • 1 Fruit • 12 Optional Calories

156 Calories • 0 gm Fat • 11 gm Protein • 28 gm Carbohydrate • 153 mg Sodium • 376 mg Calcium • 0 gm Fiber

DIABETIC EXCHANGES: 1 Fat-Free Milk • 1 Fruit

Caramel Apple Smoothie

People were almost knocking each other down in their eagerness to sample this smoothie when I announced its name in my office! We're all just kids at heart, and the idea of a caramel apple—and a healthy one at that—that you could drink was extremely appealing. Well, the idea had nothing on the actual taste—wow! This one's a star!   ☻   Serves 2 (1 cup)

> ¾ cup cold unsweetened apple juice
> 1 cup (2 small) cored, peeled, and diced apples
> 2 tablespoons Splenda Granular
> ½ teaspoon apple pie spice
> 2 tablespoons Smucker's Fat Free Caramel Syrup
> ¾ cup Dannon plain fat-free yogurt

In a blender container, combine apple juice, apples, Splenda, and apple pie spice. Cover and process on BLEND for 30 seconds. Add caramel syrup and yogurt. Re-cover and process on BLEND for 15 to 20 seconds or until mixture is smooth. Evenly pour into 2 glasses. Serve at once.

Each serving equals:

HE: 1¾ Fruit • ½ Fat-Free Milk • ½ Slider • 16 Optional Calories

---

180 Calories • 0 gm Fat • 5 gm Protein • 40 gm Carbohydrate • 128 mg Sodium • 214 mg Calcium • 2 gm Fiber

---

DIABETIC EXCHANGES: 1½ Fruit • ½ Fat-Free Milk • ½ Starch/Carbohydrate

Pineapple–Coconut Patty Smoothie

Did you ever receive a box of those coconut patties from friends who visited Hawaii? They're as difficult to resist as this smoothie, which combines the lushest fruit of the islands with that candy treat. You'll be hula-ing up and down the block with happiness!

◑ Serves 2 (1 cup)

> 1 (8-ounce) can crushed pineapple, packed in fruit juice,
>   undrained
> ¼ cup Land O Lakes Fat Free Half & Half
> 2 tablespoons Hershey's Lite Chocolate Syrup
> ½ teaspoon coconut extract
> ¾ cup Dannon plain fat-free yogurt
> 2 teaspoons flaked coconut

In a blender container, combine undrained pineapple, half & half, chocolate syrup, and coconut extract. Cover and process on BLEND for 20 seconds. Add yogurt. Re-cover and process on BLEND for 15 to 20 seconds or until mixture is smooth. Evenly pour into 2 glasses. Sprinkle 1 teaspoon coconut over top of each. Serve at once.

Each serving equals:

HE: 1 Fruit • ½ Fat-Free Milk • ½ Slider •
12 Optional Calories

141 Calories • 1 gm Fat • 7 gm Protein •
26 gm Carbohydrate • 130 mg Sodium •
250 mg Calcium • 1 gm Fiber

DIABETIC EXCHANGES: 1 Fruit • ½ Fat-Free Milk •
½ Starch/Carbohydrate

Maple Milk Shake Smoothie

Creamier than you may have thought possible, this blend is smoother than silk, softer going down than velvet, and overall an experience of such deluxe delight, you will feel like royalty! If you can't find the fat-free half & half at your store, *ask*! You'll help yourself and others at the same time.   ☻   Serves 2 (1 cup)

¼ cup Land O Lakes Fat Free Half & Half
¼ cup Log Cabin Sugar Free Maple Syrup
¼ cup Splenda Granular
1½ cups Dannon plain fat-free yogurt
½ cup crushed ice

In a blender container, combine half & half, maple syrup, Splenda, and yogurt. Cover and process on BLEND for 15 seconds. Add ice. Re-cover and process on BLEND for 15 to 20 seconds or until mixture is smooth. Evenly pour into 2 glasses. Serve at once.

Each serving equals:

HE: 1 Fat-Free Milk • ¼ Slider • 17 Optional Calories

136 Calories • 0 gm Fat • 11 gm Protein •
23 gm Carbohydrate • 221 mg Sodium •
414 mg Calcium • 0 gm Fiber

DIABETIC EXCHANGES: 1 Fat-Free Milk •
½ Starch/Carbohydrate

Pink Squirrel Smoothie

Somebody must have a lot of fun naming fancy drinks, don't you think? I mean, who thought up the crème de menthe marvel called a grasshopper? (Turn the page for my version!) I can tell you that I've never seen a pink squirrel, and I'm not sure I'd want to (in real life, anyway), but drinking one is delicious!

◐ Serves 2 (1½ cups)

> 1½ cups Dannon plain fat-free yogurt
> ¼ cup Land O Lakes Fat Free Half & Half
> ¼ cup Splenda Granular
> ¼ teaspoon almond extract
> 1 tablespoon mini chocolate chips
> 5 to 6 drops red food coloring
> ½ cup crushed ice

In a blender container, combine yogurt, half & half, Splenda, almond extract, chocolate chips, and red food coloring. Cover and process on BLEND for 20 seconds. Add ice. Re-cover and process on BLEND for 30 to 35 seconds or until mixture is smooth. Evenly pour into 2 glasses. Serve at once.

Each serving equals:

HE: 1 Fat-Free Milk • ½ Slider • 7 Optional Calories

158 Calories • 2 gm Fat • 12 gm Protein • 23 gm Carbohydrate • 172 mg Sodium • 415 mg Calcium • 0 gm Fiber

DIABETIC EXCHANGES: 1 Fat-Free Milk • ½ Starch/Carbohydrate

Grasshopper Yogurt Smoothie

My friend Barbara loves anything chocolate mint, so when she went to New Orleans as a teenager and overheard someone order grasshopper ice cream, she was an immediate fan—once she understood that no insects were involved! Instead, this is a creamy, minty, magnificent treat that looks as pretty as it tastes!

◐ Serves 2 (1¼ cups)

> 1½ cups Dannon plain fat-free yogurt
> ¼ cup Land O Lakes Fat Free Half & Half
> ¼ cup Splenda Granular
> ⅛ teaspoon mint extract
> 1 tablespoon mini chocolate chips
> 5 to 6 drops green food coloring
> ½ cup crushed ice

In a blender container, combine yogurt, half & half, Splenda, mint extract, chocolate chips, and green food coloring. Cover and process on BLEND for 20 seconds. Add ice. Re-cover and process on BLEND for 30 to 35 seconds or until mixture is smooth. Evenly pour into 2 glasses. Serve at once.

Each serving equals:

HE: 1 Fat-Free Milk • ½ Slider • 1 Optional Calorie

---

154 Calories • 2 gm Fat • 12 gm Protein •
22 gm Carbohydrate • 172 mg Sodium •
415 mg Calcium • 0 gm Fiber

DIABETIC EXCHANGES: 1 Fat-Free Milk •
½ Starch/Carbohydrate

Peppermint Fizz Smoothie

Here's a birthday party dream of a drink, a fizzy, chocolate-y, minty celebration of all that celebrations are meant to be! This one delivers lots of healthy calcium but at the same time tastes like a old-fashioned soda fountain delight! ❂ Serves 2 (1¼ cups)

> 2 tablespoons Hershey's Lite Chocolate Syrup
> 1½ cups Dannon plain fat-free yogurt
> ¼ cup Splenda Granular
> ⅛ teaspoon peppermint extract
> 1 cup cold diet ginger ale

In a blender container, combine chocolate syrup, yogurt, Splenda, peppermint extract, and diet ginger ale. Cover and process on BLEND for 25 to 30 seconds or until mixture is smooth. Evenly pour into 2 glasses. Serve at once.

Each serving equals:

HE: 1 Fat-Free Milk • ¼ Slider • 6 Optional Calories

128 Calories • 0 gm Fat • 11 gm Protein •
21 gm Carbohydrate • 176 mg Sodium •
369 mg Calcium • 0 gm Fiber

DIABETIC EXCHANGES: 1 Fat-Free Milk •
½ Starch/Carbohydrate

Almond Joy Smoothie

I invented my first Almond Joy dessert recipe quite a few years ago now, but I still like to reinvent that combination again and again. Now the tempting pleasures of chocolate, coconut, and almond join hands to invite you to run wild, without sacrificing your commitment to living healthy. Such happiness in one tall glass!

◑   Serves 2 (1 cup)

> 1½ cups Dannon plain fat-free yogurt
> ¼ cup Land O Lakes Fat Free Half & Half
> 2 tablespoons Hershey's Lite Chocolate Syrup
> ¼ cup Splenda Granular
> ½ teaspoon coconut extract
> ¼ teaspoon almond extract
> 1 teaspoon flaked coconut

In a blender container, combine yogurt, half & half, and chocolate syrup. Cover and process on BLEND for 15 seconds. Add Splenda, coconut extract, and almond extract. Re-cover and process on BLEND for 10 to 15 seconds or until mixture is smooth. Evenly pour into 2 glasses. Sprinkle ½ teaspoon coconut over top of each. Serve at once.

Each serving equals:

HE: 1 Fat-Free Milk • ½ Slider • 19 Optional Calories

152 Calories • 0 gm Fat • 12 gm Protein •
26 gm Carbohydrate • 195 mg Sodium •
416 mg Calcium • 0 gm Fiber

DIABETIC EXCHANGES: 1 Fat-Free Milk •
½ Starch/Carbohydrate

Cafe-au-Lait Smoothie

If you like cream in your coffee, and a bit of cinnamon transports you to the exotic East, then here's the smoothie with your name on it! In a world of three-dollar cups of coffee, why not blend up your own coffee-flavored drink at home—and save those extra dollars for a real vacation somewhere exotic!

◕ Serves 2 (1¼ cups)

> ½ cup Land O Lakes Fat Free Half & Half
> 1 teaspoon instant coffee crystals
> ¼ cup Splenda Granular
> ⅛ teaspoon ground cinnamon
> 1½ cups Dannon plain fat-free yogurt
> 2 tablespoons Cool Whip Lite

In a blender container, combine half & half, dry coffee crystals, Splenda, and cinnamon. Cover and process on BLEND for 15 seconds. Add yogurt. Re-cover and process on BLEND for 15 to 20 seconds or until mixture is smooth. Evenly pour into 2 glasses and top each with 1 tablespoon Cool Whip Lite and lightly sprinkle additional cinnamon on top, if desired. Serve at once.

Each serving equals:

> HE: 1 Fat-Free Milk • ½ Slider • 16 Optional Calories
>
> ---
> 144 Calories • 0 gm Fat • 12 gm Protein • 24 gm Carbohydrate • 201 mg Sodium • 464 mg Calcium • 0 gm Fiber
>
> ---
> DIABETIC EXCHANGES: 1 Fat-Free Milk • ½ Starch/Carbohydrate

Dreamy Ice-Creamy Concoctions

How does that old chant go, "I scream, you scream, we all scream for ice cream!"? Well, save your voice and delight your taste buds with any and all of these ice cream–based smoothies that are the dreamiest of healthy desserts-in-a-glass! Each one is a food-lover's fantasy, combining nutritious fruits and juices with ice cream so rich you'll never believe it's sugar-free and fat-free.

Make it mocha or banana, blueberry or peach, even cola and cherry for old-fashioned fun! Whatever you do, make them often, and celebrate with every sip.

Dreamy Ice-Creamy Concoctions

Magic Banana Mocha Smoothie

Why would I call this smoothie magic? Just one sip and you'll taste why! ☻ Serves 2 (1 cup)

> *1 cup cold fat-free milk or soy milk*
> *1 cup (1 medium) diced banana*
> *¼ cup Nesquick sugar-free chocolate drink mix*
> *1½ teaspoons instant coffee crystals*
> *¾ cup Wells' Blue Bunny sugar- and fat-free chocolate ice cream*
> *   or any sugar- and fat-free ice cream*

In a blender container, combine milk, banana, chocolate drink mix, and dry coffee crystals. Cover and process on BLEND for 15 seconds. Add ice cream. Re-cover and process on BLEND for 15 to 20 seconds or until mixture is smooth. Evenly pour into 2 glasses. Serve at once.

Each serving equals:

> HE: 1 Fruit • ¾ Fat-Free Milk • ¾ Slider •
> 2 Optional Calories
>
> ---
>
> 213 Calories • 1 gm Fat • 9 gm Protein •
> 42 gm Carbohydrate • 147 mg Sodium •
> 246 mg Calcium • 4 gm Fiber
>
> ---
>
> DIABETIC EXCHANGES: 1 Fruit •
> 1 Starch/Carbohydrate • ½ Fat-Free Milk

Banana Cookies & Cream Smoothie

Talk about a luscious evening snack! Dairy-based beverages often help you relax before bedtime, so a smoothie can be a wonderful choice. This one has a particularly lush texture, made especially rich because of the banana.   ☻   Serves 2 (1 cup)

> 1 cup (1 medium) sliced banana
> ½ cup cold fat-free milk or soy milk
> 1 cup Wells' Blue Bunny sugar- and fat-free vanilla ice cream or
>   any sugar- and fat-free ice cream
> 3 (2½-inch) chocolate graham crackers, made into coarse crumbs

In a blender container, combine banana, milk, and ice cream. Cover and process on BLEND for 20 seconds. Add graham cracker crumbs. Re-cover and process on BLEND for 5 seconds. Evenly pour into 2 glasses. Serve at once.

Each serving equals:

HE: 1 Fruit • ¾ Fat-Free Milk • ½ Bread • ½ Slider • 16 Optional Calories

---

209 Calories • 1 gm Fat • 8 gm Protein • 42 gm Carbohydrate • 146 mg Sodium • 202 mg Calcium • 2 gm Fiber

---

DIABETIC EXCHANGES: 1 Fruit • 1 Starch/Carbohydrate • ½ Fat-Free Milk

Chocolate, Peanut Butter, & Banana Smoothie

What a kid-pleaser this creamy shake is! You could serve it for an afternoon birthday party or as a special treat during a sleepover. It's high in calcium, gets in a couple of fruit servings, and even provides a healthy jolt of protein—but your children will love it because it's got all those flavors kids can't resist!

◐ Serves 2 (1 cup)

> 2 cups (2 medium) sliced bananas
> 2 tablespoons Peter Pan reduced-fat peanut butter
> ½ cup cold fat-free milk or soy milk
> ½ cup Wells' Blue Bunny sugar- and fat-free chocolate ice cream
>   or any sugar- and fat-free ice cream

In a blender container, combine bananas, peanut butter, and milk. Cover and process on BLEND for 15 seconds. Add ice cream. Re-cover and process on BLEND for 10 to 15 seconds or until mixture is smooth. Evenly pour into 2 glasses. Serve at once.

Each serving equals:

HE: 2 Fruit • 1 Protein • 1 Fat • ½ Fat-Free Milk •
½ Slider • 16 Optional Calories

270 Calories • 6 gm Fat • 12 gm Protein •
42 gm Carbohydrate • 158 mg Sodium •
200 mg Calcium • 3 gm Fiber

DIABETIC EXCHANGES: 2 Fruit •
½ Starch/Carbohydrate • ½ Meat • ½ Fat

Peanut Butter Banana Smoothie

It's one of those messy sandwiches beloved of most children, but it also was the special passion of the immortal Elvis Presley. Individually, each of these ingredients is delectable; in combination, they're something to sing about!　　❂　　Serves 2 (1 cup)

1 cup (1 medium) diced banana

1 cup cold fat-free milk or soy milk

2 tablespoons Peter Pan reduced-fat peanut butter

¾ cup Wells' Blue Bunny sugar- and fat-free vanilla ice cream or any sugar- and fat-free ice cream

In a blender container, combine banana, milk, and peanut butter. Cover and process on BLEND for 15 seconds. Add ice cream. Re-cover and process on BLEND for 15 to 20 seconds or until mixture is smooth. Evenly pour into 2 glasses. Serve at once.

Each serving equals:

HE: 1 Protein • 1 Fruit • 1 Fat • ¾ Fat-Free Milk • ¼ Slider • 15 Optional Calories

266 Calories • 6 gm Fat • 12 gm Protein • 41 gm Carbohydrate • 177 mg Sodium • 245 mg Calcium • 3 gm Fiber

DIABETIC EXCHANGES: 1 Fruit • 1 Starch/Carbohydrate • ½ Fat-Free Milk • ½ Fat • ½ Meat

Chocolate Banana Cream Smoothie

What could be tastier and more lip-smacking than the beverage equivalent of a chocolate-covered banana? This makes a satisfying dessert, a superb between-meals snack, and a definitely decadent weekend brunch component.　●　Serves 2 (1¼ cups)

> 1 cup cold fat-free milk or soy milk
> 1 cup (1 medium) diced banana
> ½ teaspoon vanilla extract
> 1 cup Wells' Blue Bunny sugar- and fat-free chocolate ice cream or any sugar- and fat-free ice cream

In a blender container, combine milk, banana, and vanilla extract. Cover and process on BLEND for 15 seconds. Add ice cream. Re-cover and process on BLEND for 15 to 20 seconds or until mixture is smooth. Evenly pour into 2 glasses. Serve at once.

Each serving equals:

HE: 1 Fat-Free Milk • 1 Fruit • ¼ Slider • 15 Optional Calories

192 Calories • 0 gm Fat • 9 gm Protein • 39 gm Carbohydrate • 114 mg Sodium • 275 mg Calcium • 2 gm Fiber

DIABETIC EXCHANGES: 1 Fruit • 1 Starch/Carbohydrate • ½ Fat-Free Milk

Banana Nog Smoothie

Why should a drink as delightful as eggnog be served only at holiday time? And why shouldn't there be nog-type drinks featuring other scrumptious flavors? My answer to the first question is, let's enjoy eggnog-style drinks all year long. And my answer to the second? This beautiful banana recipe!   ☻   Serves 4 (1 cup)

> 1½ cups cold fat-free milk or soy milk
> 2 cups (2 medium) sliced bananas
> 1½ cups Wells' Blue Bunny sugar- and fat-free vanilla ice cream
>   or any sugar- and fat-free ice cream
> ½ teaspoon rum extract
> ¼ teaspoon ground cinnamon

In a blender container, combine milk and bananas. Cover and process on BLEND for 15 seconds. Add ice cream, rum extract, and cinnamon. Re-cover and process on BLEND for 15 to 20 seconds or until mixture is smooth. Evenly pour into 4 glasses. Serve at once.

Each serving equals:

HE: 1 Fruit • ½ Fat-Free Milk • ¼ Slider •
17 Optional Calories

---

168 Calories • 0 gm Fat • 8 gm Protein •
34 gm Carbohydrate • 86 mg Sodium •
208 mg Calcium • 2 gm Fiber

DIABETIC EXCHANGES: 1 Fruit • 1 Starch/Carbohydrate

Angel Frost Smoothie

My first reaction when I sipped this smoothie was, "Heavenly!" Cool and creamy, sweet and tart, it's an enticing treat for the entire family, and perfect party food. If your blender is too small to handle the ingredients as described, this recipe will work if you halve everything (or prepare it in two batches).

◐ Serves 6 (1 full cup)

> 1 tub Crystal Light Lemonade mix
> 3 cups cold fat-free milk or soy milk
> 3 cups frozen unsweetened strawberries, partially thawed
> ¼ cup Splenda Granular
> 1½ cups Wells' Blue Bunny sugar- and fat-free vanilla ice cream
>   or any sugar- and fat-free ice cream

In a blender container, combine dry lemonade mix, milk, strawberries, and Splenda. Cover and process on BLEND for 30 seconds. Add ice cream. Re-cover and process on BLEND for 20 to 25 seconds or until mixture is smooth. Evenly pour into 6 glasses. Serve at once.

Each serving equals:

HE: ¾ Fat-Free Milk • ½ Fruit • ¼ Slider •
2 Optional Calories

---

128 Calories • 0 gm Fat • 6 gm Protein •
26 gm Carbohydrate • 89 mg Sodium •
254 mg Calcium • 2 gm Fiber

DIABETIC EXCHANGES: ½ Fat-Free Milk • ½ Fruit •
½ Starch/Carbohydrate

Creamy Strawberry Daiquiri Smoothie

This is my vote for "Pretty in Pink" and a lovely choice to serve at a wedding or engagement shower. What better way to launch a bride or fiancée on the journey of a lifetime? Besides, pink is so flattering to just every woman I know! ☻ Serves 4 (1 cup)

> 1¼ cups cold Diet Mountain Dew
> 1 (4-serving) package JELL-O sugar-free strawberry gelatin
> 2 cups frozen unsweetened strawberries
> 1 cup Wells' Blue Bunny sugar- and fat-free vanilla ice cream or
>   any sugar- and fat-free ice cream

In a blender container, combine Diet Mountain Dew and dry gelatin. Cover and process on BLEND for 20 seconds. Add strawberries. Re-cover and process on BLEND for 30 seconds. Add ice cream. Re-cover and process on BLEND for 15 to 20 seconds or until mixture is smooth. Evenly pour into 4 glasses. Serve at once.

Each serving equals:

HE: ½ Fruit • ¼ Fat-Free Milk • ¼ Slider •
1 Optional Calorie

84 Calories • 0 gm Fat • 2 gm Protein •
19 gm Carbohydrate • 39 mg Sodium •
78 mg Calcium • 2 gm Fiber

DIABETIC EXCHANGES: ½ Fruit •
½ Starch/Carbohydrate

Raspberry Chocolate Delight Smoothie

What a great "sundae-in-a-glass"! The chocolate and raspberry flavors fit perfectly together, each one making the other taste better. The drink mix adds a real "fudgy" bonus to this beverage.

○ Serves 2 (1½ cups)

> 1 cup cold fat-free milk or soy milk
> ¼ cup Nesquick sugar-free chocolate drink mix
> 1½ cups frozen unsweetened red raspberries
> ¾ cup Wells' Blue Bunny sugar- and fat-free chocolate ice cream
>   or any sugar- and fat-free ice cream

In a blender container, combine milk, chocolate drink mix, and raspberries. Cover and process on BLEND for 30 seconds. Add ice cream. Re-cover and process on BLEND for 15 to 20 seconds or until mixture is smooth. Evenly pour into 2 glasses. Serve at once.

Each serving equals:

HE: 1 Fruit • ¾ Fat-Free Milk • ¾ Slider •
17 Optional Calories

189 Calories • 1 gm Fat • 9 gm Protein •
36 gm Carbohydrate • 146 mg Sodium •
261 mg Calcium • 8 gm Fiber

DIABETIC EXCHANGES: 1 Fruit •
1 Starch/Carbohydrate • ½ Fat-Free Milk

Razzle-Dazzle Smoothie

I remember a childhood cartoon in which Tiny Tim sang about his favorite part of Christmas dinner being "razzleberry dressing," and that kind of adoration for the unique razzle-dazzle of raspberries isn't unusual. They're just that good!

○ Serves 2 (1¼ cups)

¼ cup cold fat-free milk or soy milk
¼ cup Land O Lakes Fat Free Half & Half
1 cup Wells' Blue Bunny sugar- and fat-free vanilla ice cream or
   any sugar- and fat-free ice cream
1½ cups frozen unsweetened red raspberries
½ cup cold Diet Mountain Dew

In a blender container, combine milk, half & half, and ice cream. Cover and process on BLEND for 20 seconds. Add raspberries and Diet Mountain Dew. Re-cover and process on BLEND for 15 to 20 seconds or until mixture is smooth. Evenly pour into 2 glasses. Serve at once.

Each serving equals:

HE: 1 Fruit • ¼ Fat-Free Milk • 1 Slider •
5 Optional Calories

124 Calories • 0 gm Fat • 7 gm Protein •
24 gm Carbohydrate • 70 mg Sodium •
165 mg Calcium • 6 gm Fiber

DIABETIC EXCHANGES: 1 Fruit • 1 Starch/Carbohydrate

Raspberry Almond Cream Smoothie

As nuts go, almonds are the cool, classy ones—perfect for slivering on fancy green beans or for serving at a cocktail party. So think of this smoothie as a glamorous, elegant choice, something special to serve your guests but also a way to treat yourself well.

○ Serves 2 (1 full cup)

> 1½ cups frozen unsweetened red raspberries
> 1 cup cold fat-free milk or soy milk
> ¼ teaspoon almond extract
> ½ cup Splenda Granular
> 1 cup Wells' Blue Bunny sugar- and fat-free vanilla ice cream or
>   any sugar- and fat-free ice cream
> 1 teaspoon slivered almonds

In a blender container, combine raspberries, milk, almond extract, and Splenda. Cover and process on BLEND for 20 seconds. Add ice cream. Re-cover and process on BLEND for 15 to 20 seconds or until mixture is smooth. Evenly pour into 2 glasses and top each glass with ½ teaspoon almonds. Serve at once.

Each serving equals:

HE: 1 Fat-Free Milk • 1 Fruit • ½ Slider •
2 Optional Calories

---

192 Calories • 0 gm Fat • 10 gm Protein •
38 gm Carbohydrate • 112 mg Sodium •
302 mg Calcium • 6 gm Fiber

DIABETIC EXCHANGES: 1 Starch/Carbohydrate •
1 Fruit • ½ Fat-Free Milk

Blueberry Thrill Smoothie

Am I pushing the envelope to say that a smoothie can actually be thrilling? Well, think about the sort of ordinary "diet" shakes available to people watching their weight or concerned about other health issues. By stirring in some ice cream and berries, you get a real dessert drink, a healthy reward for caring about your health!

◐ Serves 4 (1 cup)

> 1½ cups frozen unsweetened blueberries
> ½ cup Splenda Granular
> 2 cups cold fat-free milk or soy milk
> 1½ cups Wells' Blue Bunny sugar- and fat-free vanilla ice cream
>   or any sugar- and fat-free ice cream

In a blender container, combine blueberries, Splenda, and milk. Cover and process on BLEND for 20 seconds. Add ice cream. Re-cover and process on BLEND for 15 to 20 seconds or until mixture is smooth. Evenly pour into 4 glasses. Serve at once.

Each serving equals:

HE: ¾ Fat-Free Milk • ½ Fruit • ½ Slider •
9 Optional Calories

---

124 Calories • 0 gm Fat • 7 gm Protein •
29 gm Carbohydrate • 101 mg Sodium •
245 mg Calcium • 1 gm Fiber

DIABETIC EXCHANGES: ½ Fat-Free Milk • ½ Fruit •
½ Starch/Carbohydrate

Pears Helene Smoothie

Alas, no one has yet created a dessert in my honor, though I have created many for special individuals and important occasions. Pears Helene was created by a great French chef to honor the legendary Helen of Troy. She may have been "the face that launched a thousand ships," but at least we got a delicious dessert out of it!

◐ Serves 2 (1 cup)

1 (8-ounce) can pear halves, packed in fruit juice, undrained
1 cup cold fat-free milk or soy milk
1 cup Wells' Blue Bunny sugar- and fat-free chocolate ice cream or any sugar- and fat-free ice cream
2 tablespoons Cool Whip Lite
1 teaspoon mini chocolate chips

In a blender container, combine undrained pears and milk. Cover and process on BLEND for 15 seconds. Add ice cream. Re-cover and process on BLEND for 15 to 20 seconds or until mixture is smooth. Evenly pour into 2 glasses. Top each with 1 tablespoon Cool Whip Lite and ½ teaspoon chocolate chips. Serve at once.

Each serving equals:

HE: 1 Fruit • ¾ Fat-Free Milk • ¾ Slider •
9 Optional Calories

173 Calories • 1 gm Fat • 8 gm Protein •
33 gm Carbohydrate • 116 mg Sodium •
256 mg Calcium • 2 gm Fiber

DIABETIC EXCHANGES: 1 Fruit •
1 Starch/Carbohydrate • ½ Fat-Free Milk

Peach Pleasure Smoothie

When we tested this smoothie recipe, the sighs of pleasure that followed the first sips convinced me that was the perfect name for it! Peaches just have that luxuriously sweet flavor and texture, and combined with ice cream, they deliver as much pleasure as you can possibly bear! I bet my daughter, Becky, will vote this one her favorite.   ☻   Serves 4 (1½ cups)

> 1 (16-ounce) can sliced peaches, packed in fruit juice, undrained
> 2 cups cold fat-free milk or soy milk
> 1½ cups Wells' Blue Bunny sugar- and fat-free vanilla ice cream
>   or any sugar- and fat-free ice cream

In a blender container, combine undrained peaches and milk. Cover and process on BLEND for 20 seconds. Add ice cream. Re-cover and process on BLEND for 15 to 20 seconds or until mixture is smooth. Evenly pour into 4 glasses. Serve at once.

Each serving equals:

HE: 1 Fruit • ¾ Fat-Free Milk • ¼ Slider •
18 Optional Calories

180 Calories • 0 gm Fat • 7 gm Protein •
38 gm Carbohydrate • 121 mg Sodium •
241 mg Calcium • 1 gm Fiber

DIABETIC EXCHANGES: 1 Fruit • ½ Fat-Free Milk •
½ Starch/Carbohydrate

Cherry Cola Smoothie

Back in the days when we drank our cokes at the local soda fountain, a cherry coke meant a Coca-Cola with a squirt of cherry syrup in it. Later, of course, you could buy cherry-flavored colas right in the can or bottle—easier, but less romantic, somehow. So I'm returning to the original glories of this old-fashioned treat—adding my own cherries into the mix!   ☻   Serves 2 (1 cup)

¾ cup cold diet Coke
1½ cups frozen unsweetened bing or dark sweet cherries
1 cup Wells' Blue Bunny sugar- and fat-free vanilla ice cream or
   any sugar- and fat-free ice cream

In a blender container, combine diet Coke and cherries. Cover and process on BLEND for 30 seconds. Add ice cream. Re-cover and process on BLEND for 25 to 30 seconds or until mixture is smooth. Evenly pour into 2 glasses. Serve at once.

Each serving equals:

HE: 1½ Fruit • ½ Fat-Free Milk • ¼ Slider •
15 Optional Calories

160 Calories • 0 gm Fat • 5 gm Protein •
35 gm Carbohydrate • 55 mg Sodium •
139 mg Calcium • 2 gm Fiber

DIABETIC EXCHANGES: 1 Fruit • ½ Fat-Free Milk •
½ Starch/Carbohydrate

Springtime Smoothie

You can buy frozen rhubarb, but I've chosen to make this smoothie with the fresh stuff. I just think it has a great texture and flavor, so if at all possible, make it with fresh. If you find yourself having to use frozen rhubarb, follow the directions below and it will still please you very much. Happy spring!　　❍　Serves 2 (1 cup)

1 cup chopped fresh rhubarb
½ cup water
¼ cup Splenda Granular
1 cup frozen unsweetened whole strawberries
½ cup Wells' Blue Bunny sugar- and fat-free vanilla ice cream or
　　any sugar- and fat-free ice cream

In a medium saucepan, combine rhubarb and water. Cover and cook over medium heat for 6 to 8 minutes or until rhubarb is tender, stirring occasionally. Add Splenda. Mix well to combine. Place saucepan on a wire rack and let cool for at least 10 minutes. In a blender container, combine rhubarb mixture and strawberries. Cover and process on BLEND for 20 seconds. Add ice cream. Recover and process on BLEND for 20 to 25 seconds or until mixture is smooth. Evenly pour into 2 glasses. Serve at once.

HINT: Frozen rhubarb, thawed, may be used in place of fresh.

Each serving equals:

HE: 1 Vegetable • ½ Fruit • ¼ Fat-Free Milk •
¼ Slider • 9 Optional Calories

128 Calories • 0 gm Fat • 4 gm Protein •
28 gm Carbohydrate • 30 mg Sodium •
130 mg Calcium • 3 gm Fiber

DIABETIC EXCHANGES: 1 Fruit • ½ Starch/Carbohydrate

Creamy Cranberry Smoothie

These days, we can find fresh cranberries almost all year round, in all parts of the country. But if you've got a nice big freezer, consider freezing a few bags of the fresh ones for use during the cold months when they're less available and higher in price. This smoothie is a truly gorgeous color, which makes it even more fun to drink!

◑ Serves 2 (1 cup)

> 1 cup cold Ocean Spray reduced-calorie cranberry juice cocktail
> ½ cup fresh or frozen whole cranberries
> ¼ cup Splenda Granular
> 1 cup Wells' Blue Bunny sugar- and fat-free vanilla ice cream or
>   any sugar- and fat-free ice cream

In a blender container, combine cranberry juice cocktail, cranberries, and Splenda. Cover and process on BLEND for 20 seconds. Add ice cream. Re-cover and process on BLEND for 15 to 20 seconds or until mixture is smooth. Evenly pour into 2 glasses. Serve at once.

Each serving equals:

HE: ¾ Fruit • ½ Fat-Free Milk • ½ Slider •
7 Optional Calories

---

132 Calories • 0 gm Fat • 4 gm Protein •
29 gm Carbohydrate • 54 mg Sodium •
132 mg Calcium • 1 gm Fiber

DIABETIC EXCHANGES: 1 Fruit • 1 Starch/Carbohydrate

Apple Harvest Smoothie

If one a day keeps the doctor away, then this smoothie is going to keep you out of the doctor's office (except for those necessary checkups) as long as possible! You're combining apples in three—count 'em three—ways plus some splendid spice, for a beverage that tastes as good as good health feels (and that's GOOD!).

◐ Serves 2 (1 cup)

> ¾ cup unsweetened applesauce
> ½ cup cold unsweetened apple juice
> 1 cup Wells' Blue Bunny sugar- and fat-free vanilla ice cream or
>   any sugar- and fat-free ice cream
> ½ cup (1 small) cored, peeled, and diced red apple
> ¼ teaspoon apple pie spice

In a blender container, combine applesauce, apple juice, and ice cream. Cover and process on BLEND for 15 seconds. Add apple and apple pie spice. Re-cover and process on BLEND for 10 seconds or until mixture is smooth. Evenly pour into 2 glasses. Serve at once.

Each serving equals:

HE: 1¾ Fruit • ½ Fat-Free Milk • ¼ Slider •
15 Optional Calories

---

152 Calories • 0 gm Fat • 4 gm Protein •
34 gm Carbohydrate • 53 mg Sodium •
128 mg Calcium • 2 gm Fiber

DIABETIC EXCHANGES: 2 Fruit • ½ Starch/Carbohydrate

Blue Beauty Smoothie

The comedian George Carlin used to do a routine in which he insisted there just wasn't enough blue food in the world. Well, this smoothie is blue-ish, I guess—kind of a cross between blue and purple, and combining the best of both. I'm doing my best, George—hope this helps! ☺ Serves 2 (1½ cups)

> ½ cup cold unsweetened grape juice
> 1½ cups frozen unsweetened blueberries
> ½ cup cold Diet Mountain Dew
> 1 cup Wells' Blue Bunny sugar- and fat-free vanilla ice cream or
>   any sugar- and fat-free ice cream

In a blender container, combine grape juice, blueberries, and Diet Mountain Dew. Cover and process on BLEND for 20 seconds. Add ice cream. Re-cover and process on BLEND for 20 to 25 seconds or until mixture is smooth. Evenly pour into 2 glasses. Serve at once.

Each serving equals:

HE: 1½ Fruit • ½ Fat-Free Milk • ¼ Slider •
15 Optional Calories

---

176 Calories • 0 gm Fat • 5 gm Protein •
39 gm Carbohydrate • 59 mg Sodium •
135 mg Calcium • 3 gm Fiber

DIABETIC EXCHANGES: 1½ Fruit •
1 Starch/Carbohydrate

Sangria Smoothie

The Spanish wine punch I named this in honor of is a brilliant mélange of different fruits combined, of course, with red wine. We've traded in the wine for grape juice and Diet Mountain Dew, and added ice cream for a real party-style treat. You might want to float an orange slice or lime slice in each glass to make it even more festive.　❂　Serves 4 (1 cup)

1 cup cold unsweetened orange juice
1 cup cold unsweetened grape juice
½ cup cold Diet Mountain Dew
¼ teaspoon ground cinnamon
2 cups Wells' Blue Bunny sugar- and fat-free vanilla ice cream or
*　　any sugar- and fat-free ice cream*

In a blender container, combine orange juice, grape juice, Diet Mountain Dew, and cinnamon. Cover and process on BLEND for 10 seconds. Add ice cream. Re-cover and process on BLEND for 15 to 20 seconds or until mixture is smooth. Evenly pour into 4 glasses. Serve at once.

Each serving equals:

HE: 1 Fruit • ½ Fat-Free Milk • ¼ Slider • 15 Optional Calories

156 Calories • 0 gm Fat • 5 gm Protein • 34 gm Carbohydrate • 53 mg Sodium • 132 mg Calcium • 0 gm Fiber

DIABETIC EXCHANGES: 1 Fruit • 1 Starch/Carbohydrate

Pretty in Pink Smoothie

A feast for the eyes as well as for the tummy, this smoothie is as lovely as it is elegant and sweet. It's ideal for a Sweet Sixteen party or a card party with friends. ☻ Serves 2 (1¼ cups)

> 1 cup diced and seeded watermelon
> 1 cup chopped fresh strawberries
> ½ cup Wells' Blue Bunny sugar- and fat-free vanilla ice cream or any sugar- and fat-free ice cream
> ½ cup crushed ice

In a blender container, combine watermelon, strawberries, ice cream, and ice. Cover and process on BLEND for 30 to 35 seconds or until mixture is smooth. Evenly pour into 2 glasses. Serve at once.

Each serving equals:

> HE: 1½ Fruit • ¼ Fat-Free Milk • ¼ Slider •
> 18 Optional Calories
> _____
> 92 Calories • 0 gm Fat • 2 gm Protein •
> 21 gm Carbohydrate • 28 mg Sodium •
> 76 mg Calcium • 2 gm Fiber
> _____
> DIABETIC EXCHANGES: 1 Fruit • ½ Starch/Carbohydrate

Strawberry Banana Smoothie

It's one of the most popular combinations for flavored yogurts, and it makes a spectacular ice cream 'n' fruit shake! Choose the rosiest berries you can find along with the brownest, ripest bananas (they're the sweetest!).   ☻   Serves 4 (1 cup)

1 cup cold fat-free milk or soy milk
1 cup (1 medium) sliced banana
1 cup sliced fresh strawberries
1½ cups Wells' Blue Bunny sugar- and fat-free vanilla ice cream
   or any sugar- and fat-free ice cream

In a blender container, combine milk, banana, and strawberries. Cover and process on BLEND for 15 to 20 seconds. Add ice cream. Re-cover and process on BLEND for 10 to 15 seconds or until mixture is smooth. Evenly pour into 4 glasses. Serve at once.

Each serving equals:

HE: ¾ Fruit • ½ Fat-Free Milk • 18 Optional Calories

128 Calories • 0 gm Fat • 1 gm Protein •
27 gm Carbohydrate • 69 mg Sodium •
173 mg Calcium • 2 gm Fiber

DIABETIC EXCHANGES: 1 Fruit • ½ Starch/Carbohydrate

Firecracker Smoothie

Three cheers for the red, white, and blue, whether it's Fourth of July, Flag Day, or simply a day to express your pride in being an American! Marvelous party food, of course, but this is also a good choice for a family Sunday supper on the patio.

❍ Serves 2 (1½ cups)

> 1 cup frozen unsweetened strawberries
> 1½ cups cold Diet Mountain Dew
> ¾ cup frozen unsweetened blueberries
> ½ cup Wells' Blue Bunny sugar- and fat-free vanilla ice cream or
>   any sugar- and fat-free ice cream

In a blender container, combine strawberries and Diet Mountain Dew. Cover and process on BLEND for 20 seconds. Add blueberries. Re-cover and process on BLEND for 15 seconds. Add ice cream. Re-cover and process on BLEND for 15 to 20 seconds or until mixture is smooth. Evenly pour into 2 glasses. Serve at once.

Each serving equals:

HE: 1 Fruit • ¾ Fat-Free Milk • ¼ Slider •
18 Optional Calories

116 Calories • 0 gm Fat • 3 gm Protein •
26 gm Carbohydrate • 33 mg Sodium •
83 mg Calcium • 4 gm Fiber

DIABETIC EXCHANGES: 1 Fruit • ½ Fat-Free Milk •
½ Starch/Carbohydrate

Triple Red Smoothie

Red is a great color for being noticed—in fact, television audience members who want to appear on camera are encouraged to wear red! It's always signified strength and power, too—and just think of how good you'll feel after a tall glass of this one!

○ Serves 2 (1½ cups)

> 1 cup frozen unsweetened strawberries
> ¾ cup frozen unsweetened red raspberries
> 1 cup cold Ocean Spray cranberry juice cocktail
> ½ cup Wells' Blue Bunny sugar- and fat-free vanilla ice cream or
>   any sugar- and fat-free ice cream

In a blender container, combine strawberries, raspberries, and cranberry juice cocktail. Cover and process on BLEND for 15 seconds. Add ice cream. Re-cover and process on BLEND for 20 to 25 seconds or until mixture is smooth. Evenly pour into 2 glasses. Serve at once.

Each serving equals:

HE: 1½ Fruit • ¼ Fat-Free Milk • ¼ Slider • 15 Optional Calories

120 Calories • 0 gm Fat • 2 gm Protein • 28 gm Carbohydrate • 31 mg Sodium • 102 mg Calcium • 5 gm Fiber

DIABETIC EXCHANGES: 1½ Fruit • ½ Starch/Carbohydrate

Cranberry Craze Smoothie

Tart and sweet, cool and smooth, this is one smoothie worth going wild for! It looks so beautiful when you serve it, so make sure to use clear glasses to show it off.   ☻   Serves 2 (1½ cups)

> 1 cup cold Ocean Spray reduced-calorie cranberry juice cocktail
> 1 cup frozen unsweetened whole strawberries
> 1 cup Wells' Blue Bunny sugar- and fat-free vanilla ice cream or
>   any sugar- and fat-free ice cream

In a blender container, combine cranberry juice cocktail, strawberries, and ice cream. Cover and process on BLEND for 25 to 30 seconds or until mixture is smooth. Evenly pour into 2 glasses. Serve at once.

Each serving equals:

HE: 1 Fruit • ½ Fat-Free Milk • ¼ Slider • 15 Optional Calories

---

140 Calories • 0 gm Fat • 4 gm Protein • 31 gm Carbohydrate • 56 mg Sodium • 148 mg Calcium • 2 gm Fiber

---

DIABETIC EXCHANGES: 1 Fruit • 1 Starch/Carbohydrate

Peach Melba Smoothie

If you're looking for a smoothie that deserves to be a star, just like its opera diva namesake, this is the one! Enjoy it any time of the year, since it depends only on frozen fruit and a little ice cream.

◐ Serves 2 (1¼ cups)

> ¾ cup frozen unsweetened red raspberries
> 1 cup frozen unsweetened sliced peaches
> 1 cup cold Diet Mountain Dew
> ½ cup Wells' Blue Bunny sugar- and fat-free vanilla ice cream or any sugar- and fat-free ice cream

In a blender container, combine raspberries, peaches, and Diet Mountain Dew. Cover and process on BLEND for 10 seconds. Add ice cream. Re-cover and process on BLEND for 20 to 25 seconds or until mixture is smooth. Evenly pour into 2 glasses. Serve at once.

Each serving equals:

HE: 1½ Fruit • ¼ Fat-Free Milk • ¼ Slider •
15 Optional Calories

112 Calories • 0 gm Fat • 5 gm Protein •
23 gm Carbohydrate • 31 mg Sodium •
74 mg Calcium • 5 gm Fiber

DIABETIC EXCHANGES: 1½ Fruit •
½ Starch/Carbohydrate

Banana Blueberry Smoothie

I'd like to nominate this one to be the featured smoothie of any school or service academy that features the colors blue and gold! It's perfect after an afternoon spent cheering on your favorite team.

○ Serves 4 (1 cup)

> 1 cup (1 medium) sliced banana
> 1½ cups frozen unsweetened blueberries
> 1½ cups cold Diet Mountain Dew
> 1 cup Wells' Blue Bunny sugar- and fat-free vanilla ice cream or
>   any sugar- and fat-free ice cream

In a blender container, combine banana, blueberries, and Diet Mountain Dew. Cover and process on BLEND for 20 seconds. Add ice cream. Re-cover and process on BLEND for 30 to 35 seconds or until mixture is smooth. Evenly pour into 4 glasses. Serve at once.

Each serving equals:

HE: 1 Fruit • ¼ Fat-Free Milk • 17 Optional Calories

96 Calories • 0 gm Fat • 2 gm Protein •
22 gm Carbohydrate • 31 mg Sodium •
65 mg Calcium • 2 gm Fiber

DIABETIC EXCHANGES: 1 Fruit • ½ Starch/Carbohydrate

Citrus Squeeze Smoothie

It tastes like fun, but it's also a great choice if you're looking to add more fruit and nutrients to your daily menu. As long as everything you put into the blender is oh-so-cold, your smoothie will be a thriller!   ☉   Serves 4 (1 cup)

> 1½ cups cold unsweetened orange juice
> 1 cup frozen unsweetened whole strawberries
> ½ cup cold Diet Mountain Dew
> 1½ cups Wells' Blue Bunny sugar- and fat-free vanilla ice cream
>   or any sugar- and fat-free ice cream

In a blender container, combine orange juice, strawberries, and Diet Mountain Dew. Cover and process on BLEND for 30 seconds. Add ice cream. Re-cover and process on BLEND for 25 to 30 minutes or until mixture is smooth. Evenly pour into 4 glasses. Serve at once.

Each serving equals:

HE: 1 Fruit • ¼ Fat-Free Milk • ¼ Slider • 17 Optional Calories

124 Calories • 0 gm Fat • 4 gm Protein • 27 gm Carbohydrate • 40 mg Sodium • 106 mg Calcium • 1 gm Fiber

DIABETIC EXCHANGES: 1 Fruit • 1 Starch/Carbohydrate

Peach Pineapple Smoothie

P is for pep, and P is for passion, so when you combine two of the tastiest "P" fruits into one great shake, you've got the energy and the desire to live life to the fullest!   ☻   Serves 2 (1½ cups)

> 1 (8-ounce) can crushed pineapple, packed in fruit juice,
>   undrained
> ¾ cup cold Diet Mountain Dew
> 1 cup frozen unsweetened sliced peaches
> 1 cup Wells' Blue Bunny sugar- and fat-free vanilla ice cream or
>   any sugar- and fat-free ice cream

In a blender container, combine undrained pineapple and Diet Mountain Dew. Cover and process on BLEND for 15 seconds. Add peaches and ice cream. Re-cover and process on BLEND for 20 to 25 seconds or until mixture is smooth. Evenly pour into 2 glasses. Serve at once.

Each serving equals:

HE: 2 Fruit • ½ Fat-Free Milk • ¼ Slider •
14 Optional Calories

160 Calories • 0 gm Fat • 4 gm Protein •
32 gm Carbohydrate • 62 mg Sodium •
140 mg Calcium • 2 gm Fiber

DIABETIC EXCHANGES: 2 Fruit • 1 Starch/Carbohydrate

Pineapple Orange Smoothie

Just like the orange and pineapple juice bar drink called the Californian, this smoothie delivers a great big boost of liquid sunshine in every gulp! Don't forget the sunscreen, but go out and enjoy the sun.   ☻   Serves 4 (1¼ cups)

> 2 cups cold fat-free milk or soy milk
> 1 (8-ounce) can crushed pineapple, packed in fruit juice,
>   undrained
> ½ cup cold unsweetened orange juice
> 1½ cups Wells' Blue Bunny sugar- and fat-free vanilla ice cream
>   or any sugar- and fat-free ice cream

In a blender container, combine milk, undrained pineapple, and orange juice. Cover and process on BLEND for 15 seconds. Add ice cream. Re-cover and process on BLEND for 10 to 15 seconds or until mixture is smooth. Serve at once.

Each serving equals:

HE: ¾ Fat-Free Milk • ¾ Fruit • ¼ Slider • 17 Optional Calories

---

136 Calories • 0 gm Fat • 7 gm Protein • 27 gm Carbohydrate • 102 mg Sodium • 251 mg Calcium • 1 gm Fiber

---

DIABETIC EXCHANGES: 1 Fruit • ½ Fat-Free Milk • ½ Starch/Carbohydrate

Banana Grape Smoothie

I've rarely met a kid who didn't love the sweet intensity of grape juice, and the same is true about kids' appreciation of the humble banana. (My grandkids love both!) Here, I've teamed them up in a way that is bound to win fans from coast to coast!

◗ Serves 4 (1 cup)

> 1 cup (1 medium) diced banana
> 2 cups cold unsweetened grape juice
> ⅔ cup Carnation Nonfat Dry Milk Powder
> 1½ cups Wells' Blue Bunny sugar- and fat-free vanilla ice cream
>   or any sugar- and fat-free ice cream

In a blender container, combine banana, grape juice, and dry milk powder. Cover and process on BLEND for 20 seconds. Add ice cream. Re-cover and process on BLEND for 20 to 25 seconds or until mixture is smooth. Evenly pour into 4 glasses. Serve at once.

Each serving equals:

HE: 1½ Fruit • ¾ Fat-Free Milk • ¼ Slider •
17 Optional Calories

---

196 Calories • 0 gm Fat • 8 gm Protein •
41 gm Carbohydrate • 104 mg Sodium •
248 mg Calcium • 1 gm Fiber

DIABETIC EXCHANGES: 1½ Fruit • ½ Fat-Free Milk •
½ Starch/Carbohydrate

Apple Orange Smoothie

I've heard it said that you can't mix apples and oranges, but I'm willing to try! True, on their own, they're incomparable—each with a different great taste and texture. Together, however, their juices are unbeatable as featured players in a super-duper smoothie.

○ Serves 2 (1½ cups)

> ½ cup cold unsweetened apple juice
> ½ cup cold unsweetened orange juice
> 1 cup cold diet ginger ale
> 1 cup Wells' Blue Bunny sugar- and fat-free vanilla ice cream or
>   any sugar- and fat-free ice cream

In a blender container, combine apple juice, orange juice, and diet ginger ale. Cover and process on BLEND for 10 seconds. Add ice cream. Re-cover and process on BLEND for 15 to 20 seconds or until mixture is smooth. Evenly pour into 2 glasses. Serve at once.

Each serving equals:

HE: 1 Fruit • ½ Fat-Free Milk • ¼ Slider •
15 Optional Calories

---

136 Calories • 0 gm Fat • 4 gm Protein •
30 gm Carbohydrate • 71 mg Sodium •
129 mg Calcium • 0 gm Fiber

DIABETIC EXCHANGES: 1 Fruit • 1 Starch/Carbohydrate

Cranberry Cocktail Smoothie

What a great end-of-summer celebration drink, combining tart berries and the juiciest juice! You don't need a special occasion, just a gathering of friends to give thanks for simply being alive!

❂ Serves 4 (1 cup)

> *1 cup fresh or frozen cranberries*
> *1¼ cups cold Diet Mountain Dew*
> *1 cup cold unsweetened orange juice*
> *½ cup Splenda Granular*
> *1½ cups Wells' Blue Bunny sugar- and fat-free vanilla ice cream*
> *or any sugar- and fat-free ice cream*

In a blender container, combine cranberries, Diet Mountain Dew, orange juice, and Splenda. Cover and process on BLEND for 45 seconds. Add ice cream. Re-cover and process on BLEND for 25 to 30 seconds or until mixture is smooth. Evenly pour into 4 glasses. Serve at once.

Each serving equals:

HE: ¾ Fruit • ¼ Fat-Free Milk • ½ Slider • 9 Optional Calories

116 Calories • 0 gm Fat • 3 gm Protein • 26 gm Carbohydrate • 45 mg Sodium • 98 mg Calcium • 1 gm Fiber

DIABETIC EXCHANGES: 1 Starch/Carbohydrate • ½ Fruit

Pink Lassie Smoothie

What's fun for me—and, I hope, for you—is juggling ingredients in my recipes to experience different flavors, colors, textures, and tastes. Here's another way to combine two of our favorite juices, but by varying the amounts, I can offer you a little something different.

◐ Serves 2 (1 cup)

> 1 cup cold Ocean Spray reduced-calorie cranberry juice cocktail
> ¼ cup cold unsweetened orange juice
> 1 cup Wells' Blue Bunny sugar- and fat-free vanilla ice cream or
>   any sugar- and fat-free ice cream

In a blender container, combine cranberry juice cocktail, orange juice, and ice cream. Cover and process on BLEND for 15 to 20 seconds or until mixture is smooth. Evenly pour into 2 glasses. Serve at once.

Each serving equals:

HE: ¾ Fruit • ½ Fat-Free Milk • ¼ Slider •
15 Optional Calories

116 Calories • 0 gm Fat • 4 gm Protein •
25 gm Carbohydrate • 54 mg Sodium •
133 mg Calcium • 0 gm Fiber

DIABETIC EXCHANGES: 1 Starch/Carbohydrate • ½ Fruit

Decadent Orange Smoothie

I remember hearing the expression "divine decadence" in the movie musical *Cabaret*. I wonder if this kind of irresistible delight was what they had in mind! Just as Mae West said, "Too much of a good thing can be wonderful!"   ☻   Serves 2 (1 cup)

> ½ cup cold unsweetened orange juice
> 1 (11-ounce) can mandarin oranges, rinsed and drained
> 1 cup Wells' Blue Bunny sugar- and fat-free vanilla ice cream or
>   any sugar- and fat-free ice cream
> 2 tablespoons mini chocolate chips
> ½ cup crushed ice

In a blender container, combine orange juice, mandarin oranges, ice cream, and chocolate chips. Cover and process on BLEND for 15 seconds. Add ice. Re-cover and process on BLEND for 15 to 20 seconds or until mixture is smooth. Evenly pour into 2 glasses. Serve at once.

Each serving equals:

HE: 1½ Fruit • ½ Fat-Free Milk • ½ Slider •
15 Optional Calories

---

215 Calories • 3 gm Fat • 5 gm Protein •
42 gm Carbohydrate • 61 mg Sodium •
128 mg Calcium • 1 gm Fiber

DIABETIC EXCHANGES: 1½ Fruit •
1 Starch/Carbohydrate

Mexican Fiesta Smoothie

The mariachi band is playing, the sun is high in the sky, and you've been dancing up a storm—at least in your imagination! What more perfect, thirst-quenching beverage than this zesty orange shake?

☻ Serves 2 (1¼ cups)

> 1 cup cold unsweetened orange juice
> 1 (medium-sized) orange, peeled, seeds removed, and sectioned
> ¼ teaspoon ground cinnamon
> 1 cup Wells' Blue Bunny sugar- and fat-free chocolate ice cream or any sugar- and fat-free ice cream

In a blender container, combine orange juice, orange sections, and cinnamon. Cover and process on BLEND for 15 seconds. Add ice cream. Re-cover and process on BLEND for 15 to 20 seconds or until mixture is smooth. Evenly pour into 2 glasses. Serve at once.

Each serving equals:

HE: 1½ Fruit • ½ Fat-Free Milk • ¼ Slider • 15 Optional Calories

---

168 Calories • 0 gm Fat • 5 gm Protein • 37 gm Carbohydrate • 52 mg Sodium • 164 mg Calcium • 2 gm Fiber

---

DIABETIC EXCHANGES: 1½ Fruit • ½ Starch/Carbohydrate

Purple Cow Smoothie

Do you remember the old poem, about never seeing a purple cow, but that you'd rather see one than be one? I'd rather drink one than see or be one, wouldn't you?　　◑　　Serves 2 (1 cup)

> 1 cup cold unsweetened grape juice
> 1 cup Wells' Blue Bunny sugar- and fat-free vanilla ice cream or
> 　　any sugar- and fat-free ice cream

In a blender container, combine grape juice and ice cream. Cover and process on BLEND for 15 to 20 seconds or until mixture is smooth. Evenly pour into 2 glasses. Serve at once.

Each serving equals:

HE: 1 Fruit • ½ Fat-Free Milk • ¼ Slider •
15 Optional Calories

160 Calories • 0 gm Fat • 5 gm Protein •
35 gm Carbohydrate • 54 mg Sodium •
131 mg Calcium • 0 gm Fiber

DIABETIC EXCHANGES: 1 Fruit • 1 Starch/Carbohydrate

Shamrock Shake Smoothie

When you're in love, the whole world is Irish, or so it seems at the big St. Patrick's Day Parade in New York City! Even if you're not, join the fun and blend up this festive minty green shake!

◐ Serves 2 (1¼ cups)

1 cup cold fat-free milk or soy milk
1 cup Wells' Blue Bunny sugar- and fat-free vanilla ice cream or
    any sugar- and fat-free ice cream
2 tablespoons Splenda Granular
⅛ teaspoon mint extract
8 drops green food coloring

In a blender container, combine milk, ice cream, Splenda, mint extract, and green food coloring. Cover and process on BLEND for 15 to 20 seconds or until mixture is smooth. Evenly pour into 2 glasses. Serve at once.

Each serving equals:

HE: 1 Fat-Free Milk • ¼ Slider • 15 Optional Calories

124 Calories • 0 gm Fat • 8 gm Protein •
23 gm Carbohydrate • 114 mg Sodium •
271 mg Calcium • 0 gm Fiber

DIABETIC EXCHANGES: 1 Starch/Carbohydrate •
½ Fat-Free Milk

Mocha Cooler Smoothie

Even the list of ingredients makes your mouth water, doesn't it? I mean, coffee, cinnamon, vanilla, AND chocolate ice cream? Talk about inviting your taste buds to go dancing in the streets!

☻ Serves 2 (1 cup)

> *1 cup cold coffee*
> *1 teaspoon vanilla extract*
> *½ teaspoon ground cinnamon*
> *1½ cups Wells' Blue Bunny sugar- and fat-free chocolate ice cream or any sugar- and fat-free ice cream*
> *2 tablespoons Cool Whip Lite*
> *1 teaspoon mini chocolate chips*

In a blender container, combine coffee, vanilla extract, and cinnamon. Cover and process on BLEND for 2 to 3 seconds. Add ice cream. Re-cover and process on BLEND for 15 to 20 seconds or until mixture is smooth. For each serving, pour 1 cup mixture into a glass and top with 1 tablespoon Cool Whip Lite and ½ teaspoon chocolate chips. Serve at once.

Each serving equals:

HE: ½ Fat-Free Milk • ¾ Slider • 15 Optional Calories

170 Calories • 2 gm Fat • 6 gm Protein •
32 gm Carbohydrate • 78 mg Sodium •
189 mg Calcium • 0 gm Fiber

DIABETIC EXCHANGES: 1 Starch/Carbohydrate

Jamocha Smoothie

Oh, those lovely Caribbean islands, where you can sit under a shady tree and sip cool coffee drinks by the hour while the ocean waves whisper along the shore. It's a wonderful mind picture, very relaxing, just as this smoothie is, too!   ☻   Serves 2 (1 cup)

 ½ cup cold coffee
 ½ cup cold fat-free milk or soy milk
 ¼ cup Splenda Granular
 ⅛ teaspoon ground cinnamon
 1 cup Wells' Blue Bunny sugar- and fat-free chocolate ice cream or
       any sugar- and fat-free ice cream

In a blender container, combine coffee, milk, Splenda, and cinnamon. Cover and process on BLEND for 15 seconds. Add ice cream. Re-cover and process on BLEND for 15 to 20 seconds or until mixture is smooth. Evenly pour into 2 glasses. Serve at once.

Each serving equals:

HE: ¾ Fat-Free Milk • ¼ Slider • 15 Optional Calories

116 Calories • 0 gm Fat • 6 gm Protein •
23 gm Carbohydrate • 83 mg Sodium •
198 mg Calcium • 0 gm Fiber

DIABETIC EXCHANGES: 1 Starch/Carbohydrate

Blender Bonuses

I've always taken pride in giving my readers more for their hard-earned money—more flavor, more recipes, more attention to ease of preparation. This book is no exception! In addition to a delectable abundance of smoothie recipes, I've decided to include forty of my favorite blender recipes.

After all, you've already got the blender out. Why not celebrate its talents even more? You'll find dazzling dips, splendid soups, satisfying salads, more than a few main dishes, deliciously decadent desserts, and some of my best breakfast dishes sure to get your day off to a spectacular start!

When your goal is eating healthy all day long, there just isn't a more useful kitchen appliance than your handy blender!

Blender Bonuses

Quick Chili Con Queso

This tangy, spicy dip is so easy to make! If you love Mexican food but worry that the dishes you love are too high in fat to be part of a healthy lifestyle, give this a try. I like dipping baby carrots in it!

◐ Serves 8 (½ cup)

⅔ cup Carnation Nonfat Dry Milk Powder

¾ cup water

1 (4-ounce) can green chile peppers, drained

3 cups (16 ounces) cubed Velveeta Light processed cheese

2 tablespoons all-purpose flour

1 teaspoon dried parsley flakes

⅛ teaspoon black pepper

In a blender container, combine dry milk powder and water. Cover and process on BLEND for 10 seconds. Add green chile peppers, Velveeta cheese, flour, parsley flakes, and black pepper. Re-cover and process on CHOP for 30 seconds. Pour mixture into a medium saucepan sprayed with butter-flavored cooking spray. Cook over medium-low heat until mixture is smooth and heated through, stirring often.

Each serving equals:

HE: 2 Protein • ¼ Fat-Free Milk • ¼ Vegetable • 7 Optional Calories

136 Calories • 6 gm Fat • 13 gm Protein • 12 gm Carbohydrate • 996 mg Sodium • 402 mg Calcium • 0 gm Fiber

DIABETIC EXCHANGES: 2 Meat • ½ Starch/Carbohydrate

Creamy Scrambled Omelet

This may well be the richest, smoothest omelet you've ever tasted! The blender makes these eggs so frothy and light, you'll be astonished by how puffy they get during cooking.

◐ Serves 2 (½ cup)

> *3 eggs or equivalent in egg substitute*
> *2 tablespoons Land O Lakes Fat Free Half & Half*
> *2 teaspoons I Can't Believe It's Not Butter! Light Margarine*
> *¼ teaspoon lemon pepper*

In a blender container, combine eggs, half & half, margarine, and lemon pepper. Cover and process on BLEND for 30 seconds. Pour mixture into a medium skillet sprayed with butter-flavored cooking spray. Cook over medium heat until eggs are set, gently stirring occasionally.

Each serving equals:

HE: 1½ Protein • ½ Fat • 5 Optional Calories

129 Calories • 9 gm Fat • 10 gm Protein • 2 gm Carbohydrate • 184 mg Sodium • 62 mg Calcium • 0 gm Fiber

DIABETIC EXCHANGES: 1½ Meat • ½ Fat

Sweet Carrot Salad

You'll soon discover that your blender combines all kinds of ingredients so easily, you'll wonder why you waited this long to use it for more than milkshakes! Here, it chops the carrots and nuts, then wraps them in a dressing starring your favorite pickle relish and the best fat-free mayonnaise I've ever tasted!   ❤   Serves 4

> 3 cups coarsely chopped carrots
> ¼ cup dry-roasted peanuts
> 2 tablespoons sweet pickle relish
> ¼ cup Kraft fat-free mayonnaise
> Lettuce leaves

In a blender container, combine carrots and peanuts. Cover and process on CHOP for 10 seconds. Spoon carrot mixture into a medium bowl. Add pickle relish and mayonnaise. Mix well to combine. For each serving, place a lettuce leaf on a salad plate and spoon about ¾ cup salad mixture over top. Serve at once or refrigerate until ready to serve.

Each serving equals:

HE: 1½ Vegetable • ½ Fat • ¼ Protein • 17 Optional Calories

---

121 Calories • 5 gm Fat • 3 gm Protein • 16 gm Carbohydrate • 216 mg Sodium • 32 mg Calcium • 4 gm Fiber

---

DIABETIC EXCHANGES: 1½ Vegetable • 1 Fat • ½ Starch/Carbohydrate

Glorified Tomato Aspic

If you grew up in the 1950s, vegetable aspics were a homemaker's pride, and many home cooks created all kinds of clever variations and ways to make a vegetable gelatin salad. Now, half a century later, this glorious tomato-y dish looks pretty and tastes great!

● Serves 6

> 1 cup hot reduced-sodium tomato juice
> 1 (4-serving) package JELL-O sugar-free lemon gelatin
> ½ cup cold reduced-sodium tomato juice
> 2 tablespoons apple cider vinegar
> 1 cup diced celery
> ¼ cup chopped onion
> ¼ cup pimiento-stuffed green olives

In a blender container, combine hot tomato juice and dry gelatin. Cover and process on BLEND for 15 seconds or until gelatin is dissolved. Add cold tomato juice, vinegar, celery, onion, and olives. Re-cover and process on CHOP for 15 seconds. Pour mixture into an 8-by-8-inch dish. Refrigerate until firm, about 3 hours. Cut into 6 servings.

HINT: If desired, serve aspic on lettuce leaves and garnish with fat-free mayonnaise.

Each serving equals:

HE: ¾ Vegetable • 13 Optional Calories

24 Calories • 0 gm Fat • 1 gm Protein •
5 gm Carbohydrate • 238 mg Sodium •
17 mg Calcium • 1 gm Fiber

DIABETIC EXCHANGES: 1 Vegetable

Congealed Winter Waldorf Salad

You can now enjoy your traditional Waldorf salad in a way that works all year long, but especially in the winter months! This version is fruitier than the original, but still worthy of one of New York City's greatest hotels. ◑ Serves 6

> 2 cups Ocean Spray reduced-calorie cranberry juice cocktail ☆
> 1 (4-serving) package JELL-O sugar-free strawberry gelatin
> 2 cups (4 small) cored, unpeeled, and coarsely chopped Red
>   Delicious apples
> ¾ cup coarsely chopped celery
> ¼ cup (1 ounce) chopped walnuts

In a small saucepan, bring 1 cup cranberry juice cocktail to boiling point. In a blender container, combine boiling cranberry juice cocktail and dry gelatin. Cover and process on BLEND for 30 seconds. Add remaining 1 cup cranberry juice cocktail, apples, celery, and walnuts. Re-cover and process on CHOP for 10 seconds. Pour mixture into an 8-by-8-inch dish. Refrigerate until firm, about 3 hours. Cut into 6 servings.

HINT: Good served with 1 tablespoon Cool Whip Lite. If using, don't forget to count the few additional calories.

Each serving equals:

HE: 1 Fruit • ⅓ Fat • ¼ Vegetable •
12 Optional Calories

71 Calories • 3 gm Fat • 1 gm Protein •
10 gm Carbohydrate • 19 mg Sodium •
21 mg Calcium • 2 gm Fiber

DIABETIC EXCHANGES: 1 Fruit • ½ Fat

Pimiento-Cheddar Cheese Dip

What's a party without a few festive dips, right? But too often party dips are heavy on the sour cream and full-fat mayo, betraying our efforts to live a healthy lifestyle. Here's my way of adding pizzazz to a party without destroying anyone's diet!

◐ Serves 6 (scant ¼ cup)

> ½ cup Kraft fat-free mayonnaise
> 1 (2-ounce) jar chopped pimiento, undrained
> 1½ teaspoons Worcestershire sauce
> 1 teaspoon prepared yellow mustard
> 1 cup + 2 tablespoons (4½ ounces) shredded Kraft reduced-fat
>   Cheddar cheese
> 1 teaspoon dried parsley flakes

In a blender container, combine mayonnaise, undrained pimiento, Worcestershire, and mustard. Cover and process on BLEND for 25 seconds or until mixture is smooth. Add Cheddar cheese and parsley flakes. Re-cover and process on CHOP for 20 seconds. Spoon mixture into serving bowl. Mix well to combine. Cover and refrigerate for at least 30 minutes. Gently stir again just before serving.

Each serving equals:

HE: 1 Protein • 13 Optional Calories

---

85 Calories • 5 gm Fat • 6 gm Protein •
4 gm Carbohydrate • 185 mg Sodium •
168 mg Calcium • 0 gm Fiber

DIABETIC EXCHANGES: 1 Meat

Swiss Cheese Dip

It's just too difficult to chop a chunk of Swiss cheese finely without using a blender! But when you do use yours, the results are worth more than a yodel or two. Try this on celery or blanched string beans for a true taste treat.   ☻   Serves 6 (full ¼ cup)

> 1 cup fat-free cottage cheese
> ½ cup Kraft fat-free mayonnaise
> 2 teaspoons dried onion flakes
> ⅛ teaspoon black pepper
> 4 (¾-ounce) slices Kraft reduced-fat Swiss cheese, torn into small
>   pieces

In a blender container, combine cottage cheese, mayonnaise, onion flakes, and black pepper. Cover and process on BLEND for 20 seconds or until mixture is smooth. Add Swiss cheese pieces. Re-cover and process on CHOP for 10 seconds. Spoon mixture into serving bowl. Cover and refrigerate for at least 30 minutes. Gently stir again just before serving.

Each serving equals:

HE: 1 Protein • 13 Optional Calories

---

83 Calories • 3 gm Fat • 9 gm Protein • 5 gm Carbohydrate • 437 mg Sodium • 155 mg Calcium • 0 gm Fiber

---

DIABETIC EXCHANGES: 1 Meat

Tuna Seaside Dip

Invite the bridge club over for lunch and serve them this fresh-from-the-beach-tasting dip that you can whip up in just seconds! It's best when you let the flavors combine in the fridge for at least a half hour, and it's even better when you give it a bit longer.

🅞 Serves 8 (¼ cup)

1 (8-ounce) package Philadelphia fat-free cream cheese
1 (6-ounce) can white tuna, packed in water, drained and flaked
2 tablespoons sweet pickle relish
¼ cup Kraft fat-free mayonnaise
⅛ teaspoon black pepper

Cut cream cheese into cubes. In a blender container, combine cream cheese cubes, tuna, pickle relish, mayonnaise, and black pepper. Cover and process on BLEND for 20 seconds. (If a softer mixture is desired, add 2 tablespoons fat-free milk.) Spoon mixture into serving bowl. Cover and refrigerate for at least 30 minutes. Gently stir again just before serving.

Each serving equals:

HE: 1 Protein • 8 Optional Calories

61 Calories • 1 gm Fat • 9 gm Protein •
4 gm Carbohydrate • 311 mg Sodium •
84 mg Calcium • 0 gm Fiber

DIABETIC EXCHANGES: 1 Meat

Spanish Mayonnaise

Here's a homemade dip that is great to have on hand. It's wonderfully savory, with a real bit of tangy heat. Spread this on a sandwich and you may just start to flamenco dance in the kitchen!

◐ Serves 8 (3 tablespoons)

> 1½ cups Kraft fat-free mayonnaise
> 3 tablespoons chili sauce
> 1 teaspoon dried parsley flakes
> ½ cup (2 ounces) chopped ripe olives

In a blender container, combine mayonnaise, chili sauce, and parsley flakes. Cover and process on BLEND for 30 seconds. Add olives. Re-cover and process on CHOP for 10 seconds. Spoon mixture into container. Cover and refrigerate for at least 30 minutes. Gently stir again just before serving.

HINT: Good served with beef.

Each serving equals:

HE: ¼ Fat • ½ Slider

50 Calories • 2 gm Fat • 0 gm Protein • 8 gm Carbohydrate • 519 mg Sodium • 12 mg Calcium • 1 gm Fiber

DIABETIC EXCHANGES: ½ Fat • ½ Starch/Carbohydrate

Cucumber Sauce

This is a sauce that would be nearly impossible to prepare without the help of a blender. With the kitchen assistance of your motorized assistant chef, you've got a cool and creamy sauce that works beautifully on fresh seafood and also on salad greens.

◐ Serves 4 (¼ cup)

> *1 cup diced unpeeled cucumber*
> *1 tablespoon lemon juice*
> *⅓ cup Land O Lakes no-fat sour cream*
> *⅓ cup Kraft fat-free mayonnaise*
> *¼ teaspoon celery salt*
> *1 teaspoon dried onion flakes*

In a blender container, combine cucumber and lemon juice. Cover and process on BLEND for 30 seconds. Add sour cream, mayonnaise, celery salt, and onion flakes. Re-cover and process on BLEND for 15 seconds. Cover and refrigerate for at least 1 hour. Gently stir again just before serving.

Each serving equals:

HE: ½ Vegetable • ¼ Slider • 15 Optional Calories

36 Calories • 0 gm Fat • 1 gm Protein •
8 gm Carbohydrate • 278 mg Sodium •
33 mg Calcium • 1 gm Fiber

DIABETIC EXCHANGES: ½ Vegetable •
½ Starch/Carbohydrate

Garden-Fresh Sandwich Spread

Why pay extra money for store-made prepared sandwich spreads, which sit around for hours, even days, after they're stirred up in a commercial kitchen? Here's a good way to create one of your own that delivers all the luscious flavors of the garden!

● Serves 4 (⅓ cup)

> ⅓ cup Kraft Fat Free French Dressing
> ¾ cup (3 ounces) shredded Kraft reduced-fat Cheddar cheese
> ½ cup coarsely chopped unpeeled cucumber
> ½ cup coarsely chopped carrots
> 1½ tablespoons chopped fresh parsley or ¾ teaspoon dried
>   parsley flakes

In a blender container, combine French dressing, Cheddar cheese, cucumber, carrots, and parsley. Cover and process on BLEND for 60 seconds or until vegetables are chopped and blended.

HINT: Good as a sandwich filling or spread on crackers.

Each serving equals:

HE: 1 Protein • ½ Vegetable • ¼ Slider •
5 Optional Calories

109 Calories • 5 gm Fat • 6 gm Protein •
10 gm Carbohydrate • 205 mg Sodium •
171 mg Calcium • 1 gm Fiber

DIABETIC EXCHANGES: 1 Meat • ½ Vegetable

Bacon and Tomato Spread

Cliff might describe this recipe as a handy-dandy whiz at making sandwiches faster than the wind at night across the Iowa plains! With the talented help of your blender, this spread is ready in just seconds.   ○   Serves 8 (¼ cup)

> 2 (8-ounce) packages Philadelphia fat-free cream cheese
> 1 cup peeled and chopped fresh ripe tomato
> 1 teaspoon prepared yellow mustard
> 2 tablespoons Kraft fat-free mayonnaise
> ¼ cup Hormel Bacon Bits
> 1 tablespoon chopped fresh parsley or 1 teaspoon dried parsley
> flakes

Cut cream cheese into cubes. In a blender container, combine cream cheese cubes, tomato, mustard, and mayonnaise. Cover and process on CHOP for 10 seconds on pulse or until mixture is smooth. Add bacon bits and parsley flakes. Re-cover and process on CHOP for 5 seconds.

HINT: Good as a sandwich spread, spread on crackers, or as a dip for fresh vegetables.

Each serving equals:

HE: 1 Protein • ¼ Vegetable • 15 Optional Calories

65 Calories • 1 gm Fat • 8 gm Protein •
6 gm Carbohydrate • 444 mg Sodium •
163 mg Calcium • 0 gm Fiber

DIABETIC EXCHANGES: 1 Meat • ½ Vegetable

Pronto Chicken Spread

This is a wonderful way to get young kids to enjoy chicken salad, since you've smoothed it out and made it special! If you're not in the habit of using canned chicken, give it a chance as an alternative to tuna.　　◐　　Serves 4 (¼ cup)

> ¼ cup Kraft fat-free mayonnaise
> 1 (2-ounce) jar chopped pimiento, drained
> ½ cup chopped celery
> 1 cup (5 ounces) diced cooked chicken breast flaked
> 1 teaspoon dried parsley flakes
> ⅛ teaspoon black pepper

In a blender container, combine mayonnaise, pimiento, celery, chicken, parsley flakes, and black pepper. Cover and process on CHOP for 20 seconds.

HINT: Good as a sandwich filling or on crackers.

Each serving equals:

HE: 1¼ Protein • ¼ Vegetable • 10 Optional Calories

74 Calories • 2 gm Fat • 11 gm Protein •
3 gm Carbohydrate • 161 mg Sodium •
14 mg Calcium • 1 gm Fiber

DIABETIC EXCHANGES: 1 Meat

Festive Cranberry Relish

Not only does this look and taste delicious, your entire kitchen will be perfumed by the tart and citrusy scents of the fruits! It's especially nice with pork and turkey (those great white meats!), and I know a few people who love the taste so much, they just nibble it from the bowl. ☻ Serves 4 (⅓ cup)

¼ cup cold water
1½ cups Splenda Granular
1 (medium-sized) unpeeled seedless navel orange, cut into 12
   pieces
2 cups fresh or frozen cranberries

In a blender container, combine water, Splenda, and orange pieces. Cover and process on CHOP for 15 seconds. Add cranberries. Re-cover and process on BLEND for 20 seconds or until cranberries are chopped but not liquefied. Cover and refrigerate for at least 30 minutes. Gently stir again just before serving.

Each serving equals:

HE: ¾ Fruit • ¼ Slider • 4 Optional Calories

68 Calories • 0 gm Fat • 0 gm Protein •
17 gm Carbohydrate • 1 mg Sodium •
17 mg Calcium • 3 gm Fiber

DIABETIC EXCHANGES: 1 Fruit

Cantonese Sweet-Sour Sauce

Instead of ordering in all the time, use your blender to stir up a little taste of the exotic East in your very own home! If you've ever wondered how the restaurants combine ingredients to make sweet and sour sauces, here's your chance to learn just how!

◑ Serves 4 (full ¼ cup)

> 1 (8-ounce) can apricots, packed in fruit juice, undrained
> ¼ cup white distilled vinegar
> ½ cup Splenda Granular
> ¼ teaspoon ground ginger

In a blender container, combine apricots, vinegar, Splenda, and ginger. Cover and process on BLEND for 15 seconds or until mixture is smooth. Cover and refrigerate for at least 1 hour. Gently stir again just before serving.

HINT: Good with shrimp, ham, or pork.

Each serving equals:

HE: ½ Fruit • 8 Optional Calories

24 Calories • 0 gm Fat • 0 gm Protein • 6 gm Carbohydrate • 6 mg Sodium • 5 mg Calcium • 1 gm Fiber

DIABETIC EXCHANGES: ½ Fruit

Strawberry-Marshmallow Sauce

We're already lucky enough to have remarkably good sugar-free and fat-free ice creams available to us, but let's face it: Life is more fun when you can top that frosty scoop with a luscious sauce! Here's one I just love, but of course it features my beloved berries.

◐ Serves 4 (½ cup)

> *2 cups frozen unsweetened strawberries, slightly thawed*
> *¼ cup Diet Mountain Dew*
> *½ cup Splenda Granular*
> *¾ cup miniature marshmallows*

In a blender container, combine strawberries, Diet Mountain Dew, Splenda, and marshmallows. Cover and process on BLEND for 30 seconds or until mixture is smooth.

HINT: Wonderful spooned over sugar- and fat-free ice cream or angel food cake.

Each serving equals:

HE: ½ Fruit • ¼ Slider • 11 Optional Calories

80 Calories • 0 gm Fat • 0 gm Protein •
20 gm Carbohydrate • 8 mg Sodium •
18 mg Calcium • 2 gm Fiber

DIABETIC EXCHANGES: ½ Fruit •
½ Starch/Carbohydrate.

Cream of Vegetable Soup

If you've never learned how to use your blender as a soup "chef," here's the chance you've been waiting for! This recipe is a terrific way to boost calcium, get your veggies, and satisfy that empty tummy—all at once! ❂ Serves 4 (about 1 cup)

> 2 cups fat-free milk or soy milk
> ½ cup Land O Lakes Fat Free Half & Half
> 3 tablespoons all-purpose flour
> 1 tablespoon + 1 teaspoon I Can't Believe It's Not Butter!
>   Light Margarine
> ⅛ teaspoon black pepper
> 1 teaspoon dried parsley flakes
> 1 cup coarsely diced cooked vegetables

In a blender container, combine milk, half & half, and flour. Cover and process on BLEND for 30 seconds. Add margarine, black pepper, parsley flakes, and vegetables. Re-cover and process on BLEND for 1 to 2 minutes or until mixture is smooth. Pour mixture into a medium saucepan sprayed with butter-flavored cooking spray. Cook over medium-low heat until mixture is heated through, stirring constantly.

Each serving equals:

HE: ½ Fat-Free Milk • ½ Fat • ½ Vegetable • ¼ Bread

102 Calories • 2 gm Fat • 6 gm Protein • 15 gm Carbohydrate • 171 mg Sodium • 199 mg Calcium • 1 gm Fiber

DIABETIC EXCHANGES: ½ Fat-Free Milk • ½ Fat • ½ Vegetable • ½ Starch

VARIATIONS: 1. 1 (8-ounce) can asparagus, rinsed and drained, and ½ teaspoon prepared yellow mustard.
2. 1 (8-ounce) can whole-kernel corn, rinsed and drained, 1 teaspoon dried onion flakes, and 2 tablespoons Hormel Bacon Bits.
3. 1 (4.5-ounce) can sliced mushrooms, 2 teaspoons dried onion flakes, and ¼ teaspoon celery seed.
4. 1 (8-ounce) can spinach, rinsed and drained, and ⅛ teaspoon ground nutmeg.

Cream of Carrot Soup

A feast for the eyes as well as the appetite, this soup is one of the prettiest I've ever prepared! This is my idea of the right way to use healthy convenience foods to create a dish good enough to serve your guests. ☻ Serves 4 (scant 1 cup)

> 1 (12-fluid-ounce) can Carnation Evaporated Fat-Free Milk
> ½ cup Land O Lakes Fat Free Half & Half
> 1 (16-ounce) can sliced carrots, rinsed and drained
> 3 tablespoons all-purpose flour
> 1 tablespoon + 1 teaspoon I Can't Believe It's Not Butter! Light Margarine
> 1½ teaspoons dried onion flakes
> 1 teaspoon dried parsley flakes
> ¼ teaspoon ground ginger

In a blender container, combine evaporated milk, half & half, and carrots. Cover and process on BLEND for 30 seconds. Add flour, margarine, onion flakes, parsley flakes, and ginger. Re-cover and process on BLEND for 10 seconds or until mixture is smooth. Pour mixture into a medium saucepan sprayed with butter-flavored cooking spray. Cook over medium-low heat for 5 minutes or until mixture is heated through, stirring often using a wire whisk.

Each serving equals:

HE: 1 Vegetable • ¾ Fat-Free Milk • ½ Fat • ¼ Bread • ¼ Slider

---

158 Calories • 2 gm Fat • 9 gm Protein • 26 gm Carbohydrate • 446 mg Sodium • 312 mg Calcium • 2 gm Fiber

---

DIABETIC EXCHANGES: 1 Vegetable • 1 Fat-Free Milk • ½ Fat • ½ Starch/Carbohydrate

Cream of Pea and Chicken Soup

I admit it, this is a slightly unusual combination, but sometimes it's the right thing to take "the road less traveled," as Robert Frost reminded us. Peas and chicken turn out to be a wonderful blend, not unlike the flavor you may have encountered in chicken pot pies over the years.   ☻   Serves 4 (1 cup)

1½ cups frozen peas, thawed
1 (16-ounce) can Healthy
    Request Chicken Broth
½ cup Land O Lakes Fat Free
    Half & Half
1 tablespoon + 1 teaspoon I
    Can't Believe It's Not
    Butter! Light Margarine

3 tablespoons all-purpose flour
⅛ teaspoon black pepper
1 (5-ounce) can Hormel
    97% Fat Free Breast of
    Chicken, packed in water,
    drained and flaked
1 tablespoon dried onion flakes

In a blender container, combine peas and chicken broth. Cover and process on BLEND for 30 seconds. Add half & half, margarine, flour, and black pepper. Re-cover and process on BLEND for 15 to 20 seconds or until mixture is smooth. Pour mixture into a medium saucepan sprayed with butter-flavored cooking spray. Stir in chicken and onion flakes. Cook over medium-low heat for 5 to 6 minutes or until mixture is heated through, stirring often.

HINT: Thaw peas by placing in a colander and rinsing under hot water for one minute.

Each serving equals:

HE: 1¼ Protein • 1 Bread • ½ Fat • ¼ Slider •
9 Optional Calories

159 Calories • 3 gm Fat • 17 gm Protein •
16 gm Carbohydrate • 371 mg Sodium •
69 mg Calcium • 3 gm Fiber

DIABETIC EXCHANGES: 1 Meat • 1 Starch • ½ Fat

Fresh Tomato Cream Soup

I'm a woman who loves her garden, and I've just about always raised tomatoes in it. I use fresh tomatoes in so many ways. A fresh tomato soup is a taste treat challenging to describe but absolutely irresistible once you've tried it! Buy the tomatoes to make this recipe, then start digging up some nearby dirt—you're going to want your own tomato plants very soon. ☺ Serves 4 (1 full cup)

1 (12-fluid-ounce) can Carnation Evaporated Fat-Free Milk

3 cups peeled and coarsely chopped fresh tomatoes

½ cup chopped onion

1 tablespoon all-purpose flour

2 tablespoons chopped fresh parsley or 2 teaspoons dried parsley flakes

1 tablespoon Splenda Granular

⅛ teaspoon black pepper

1 tablespoon + 1 teaspoon I Can't Believe It's Not Butter! Light Margarine

In a blender container, combine evaporated milk, tomatoes, and onion. Cover and process on CHOP for 30 seconds. Add flour, parsley, Splenda, and black pepper. Re-cover and process on BLEND for 30 to 40 seconds, or until mixture is smooth. Pour mixture into a medium saucepan sprayed with butter-flavored cooking spray. Add margarine. Cook over medium-low heat for 6 minutes or until mixture is heated through, stirring often.

Each serving equals:

HE: 1¾ Vegetable • ¾ Fat-Free Milk • ½ Fat • 9 Optional Calories

134 Calories • 2 gm Fat • 7 gm Protein • 22 gm Carbohydrate • 179 mg Sodium • 255 mg Calcium • 2 gm Fiber

DIABETIC EXCHANGES: 1½ Vegetable • 1 Fat-Free Milk • ½ Fat

Easy Vichyssoise

Good doesn't have to mean difficult or time-consuming, although the original method of preparing this French potato soup takes a very long time. But I think you'll discover that my blender version has plenty of intense potato flavor, and the texture is truly magnificent. ☻ Serves 4 (1 cup)

> 1 (16-ounce) can Healthy Request Chicken Broth
> ½ cup water
> ⅓ cup Carnation Nonfat Dry Milk Powder
> ½ cup Land O Lakes Fat Free Half & Half
> 1 cup (2¼ ounces) instant potato flakes
> ½ cup (4 ounces) Philadelphia fat-free cream cheese, cubed
> 1 tablespoon freeze-dried chives
> ⅛ teaspoon black pepper
> ¼ cup diced cucumber, optional
> ¼ cup chopped fresh tomato, optional

In a blender container, combine chicken broth, water, and dry milk powder. Cover and process on BLEND for 10 seconds. Add half & half, potato flakes, cream cheese, chives, and black pepper. Re-cover and process on BLEND for 30 to 40 seconds or until mixture is smooth. Pour 1 cup of mixture into 4 small soup bowls. Cover and refrigerate for at least 30 minutes. When serving, garnish each with 1 tablespoon cucumber and 1 tablespoon tomato, if desired.

Each serving equals:

HE: ¾ Bread • ½ Protein • ¼ Fat-Free Milk •
¼ Vegetable • ¼ Slider • 9 Optional Calories

100 Calories • 0 gm Fat • 9 gm Protein •
16 gm Carbohydrate • 418 mg Sodium •
205 mg Calcium • 0 gm Fiber

DIABETIC EXCHANGES: 1 Starch/Carbohydrate • ½ Meat

Cold Cranberry Soup

What a summery delight, the rosiest of cool seasonal appetizers—and it's just as good with frozen berries as with fresh. (The cranberry freezes better than many fruits, and it doesn't get mushy over time.)   ☻   Serves 4 (¾ cup)

> 2 cups fresh or frozen cranberries
> 1¼ cups Splenda Granular
> 1 tablespoon Quick Cooking Minute Tapioca
> ¼ teaspoon ground cinnamon
> 2 cups Diet Mountain Dew
> ¼ cup Cool Whip Lite

In a medium saucepan, combine cranberries, Splenda, tapioca, cinnamon, and Diet Mountain Dew. Cook over medium heat for 10 minutes or until cranberries soften and burst, stirring often. Pour hot mixture into blender container. Cover and process on BLEND for 30 seconds, or until mixture is smooth. Evenly pour into 4 decorative soup bowls and refrigerate for at least 30 minutes. When serving, top each with 1 tablespoon Cool Whip Lite.

Each serving equals:

HE: ½ Fruit • ½ Slider • 1 Optional Calorie

68 Calories • 0 gm Fat • 0 gm Protein • 17 gm Carbohydrate • 12 mg Sodium • 4 mg Calcium • 2 gm Fiber

DIABETIC EXCHANGES: ½ Fruit • ½ Starch/Carbohydrate

Popovers

Blenders are ideal for making super-fast and smooth batters for baking, especially as demonstrated in this somewhat unusual popover recipe. Served with a bit of spreadable fruit, these are simply spectacular. ❂ Serves 6 (1 each)

1 cup water

⅓ cup Carnation Nonfat Dry Milk Powder

2 eggs or equivalent in egg substitute

1 tablespoon I Can't Believe It's Not Butter! Light Margarine

1 cup + 2 tablespoons all-purpose flour

¼ teaspoon table salt

Preheat oven to 425 degrees. Spray 6 (6-ounce) custard cups with butter-flavored cooking spray. In a blender container, combine water, dry milk powder, and eggs. Cover and process on BLEND for 15 seconds. Add margarine, flour, and salt. Re-cover and process on BLEND for 20 seconds, or until mixture is smooth. Pour mixture evenly into prepared custard cups. Arrange custard cups on a baking sheet. Bake for 22 to 26 minutes or until popovers are puffed and brown. Pierce the side of each popover with a sharp knife to allow steam to escape. Serve at once.

Each serving equals:

HE: 1 Bread • ⅓ Protein • ¼ Fat •
15 Optional Calories

131 Calories • 3 gm Fat • 6 gm Protein •
20 gm Carbohydrate • 162 mg Sodium •
62 mg Calcium • 1 gm Fiber

DIABETIC EXCHANGES: 1½ Starch

Fritter Potato Pancakes

If you've loved potato fritters all your life (and most of us Midwesterners admit to such a passion), here's a smart way to enjoy the flavor you love in a slightly different format! These aren't greasy, they taste of all the good ingredients and spices you've added in, and they bring a smile to every kid's face in the room.

☺ Serves 4 (2 each)

> ¼ cup fat-free milk or soy milk
> 2 eggs or equivalent in egg substitute
> ½ cup chopped onion
> 6 tablespoons all-purpose flour
> ½ teaspoon baking powder
> ½ teaspoon table salt
> 1½ cups (5 ounces) shredded loose-packed frozen potatoes,
>   slightly thawed

In a blender container, combine milk, eggs, onion, flour, baking powder, and salt. Cover and process on BLEND for 30 seconds. Add shredded potatoes. Re-cover and process on BLEND for 10 seconds. Using a ¼ cup measuring cup as a guide, spoon batter onto a hot griddle or skillet sprayed with butter-flavored cooking spray to form 8 pancakes. Cook for 3 to 4 minutes on each side or until pancakes are browned.

Each serving equals:

HE: ¾ Bread • ½ Protein • 6 Optional Calories

---

110 Calories • 2 gm Fat • 6 gm Protein •
17 gm Carbohydrate • 101 mg Sodium •
74 mg Calcium • 1 gm Fiber

DIABETIC EXCHANGES: 1 Starch • ½ Meat

Apple Appeal Flapjacks

Don't you sometime wonder about the origin of the word *flapjack*? I was curious, imagining some pioneer cook on the way west who did his best to produce a tasty breakfast for all those families traveling to California around the time of the gold rush. They may not have found gold, but in these golden fritters they find a special magic.   ☻   Serves 4 (2 each)

⅓ cup Carnation Nonfat Dry Milk Powder

¾ cup water

1 cup (2 small) cored, peeled, and coarsely chopped apples

1 egg or equivalent in egg substitute

1 tablespoon Splenda Granular

2 tablespoons I Can't Believe It's Not Butter! Light Margarine

¼ teaspoon ground cinnamon

¾ cup Bisquick Reduced Fat Baking Mix

In a blender container, combine dry milk powder, water, apples, egg, Splenda, margarine, and cinnamon. Cover and process on BLEND for 10 seconds, or until apple is grated. Add baking mix. Re-cover and process on BLEND for 15 seconds or until mixture is smooth. Using a ¼ cup measuring cup as a guide, pour batter onto a hot griddle or skillet sprayed with butter-flavored cooking spray to form 8 pancakes. Cook for 3 to 4 minutes or until pancakes are browned on both sides.

Each serving equals:

HE: 1 Bread • ½ Fruit • ¼ Fat-Free Milk •
¼ Protein • ¼ Fat • 1 Optional Calorie

---

152 Calories • 4 gm Fat • 5 gm Protein •
24 gm Carbohydrate • 331 mg Sodium •
108 mg Calcium • 1 gm Fiber

DIABETIC EXCHANGES: 1½ Starch/Carbohydrate •
½ Fruit • ½ Fat

Orange Pecan Pancakes

I love making pancakes in the blender, and I'm confident you will agree it's a great way to go. This recipe is a recent favorite of mine because the orange flavor is so incredible. It sort of makes you want to curl up on the sofa and dream of Florida oranges.

◐ Serves 6 (1 each)

> 1 cup unsweetened orange juice
> ⅓ cup Carnation Nonfat Dry Milk Powder
> 1 egg or equivalent in egg substitute
> 2 tablespoons Splenda Granular
> 1 cup + 2 tablespoons Bisquick Reduced Fat Baking Mix
> 3 tablespoons (¾ ounce) chopped pecans

In a blender container, combine orange juice and dry milk powder. Cover and process on BLEND for 10 seconds. Add egg, Splenda, and baking mix. Re-cover and process on BLEND for 30 seconds. Add pecans. Re-cover and process on BLEND for 5 seconds. Using a ⅓ cup measuring cup as a guide, pour batter onto a hot griddle or skillet sprayed with butter-flavored cooking spray to form 6 pancakes. Cook for 3 to 4 minutes or until browned on both sides.

Each serving equals:

> HE: 1 Bread • ½ Fat • ⅓ Fruit • ¼ Slider •
> 7 Optional Calories
>
> ---
>
> 153 Calories • 5 gm Fat • 4 gm Protein •
> 23 gm Carbohydrate • 293 mg Sodium •
> 83 mg Calcium • 1 gm Fiber
>
> ---
>
> DIABETIC EXCHANGES: 1½ Starch/Carbohydrate • ½ Fat

Quiche Lorraine

No French chef would dare be without a quiche recipe, and this one is terrifically easy. By including some ready-made items like the pie crust and the pre-cooked bacon, you speed up the preparation process. ☻ Serves 8

1 Pillsbury refrigerated unbaked 9-inch pie crust

¼ cup Hormel Bacon Bits

4 (¾-ounce) slices Kraft reduced-fat Swiss cheese, shredded

2 eggs or equivalent in egg substitute

3 tablespoons all-purpose flour

⅛ teaspoon black pepper

⅛ teaspoon ground nutmeg

1 (12-fluid-ounce) can Carnation Evaporated Fat-Free Milk

½ cup Land O Lakes Fat Free Half & Half

¼ cup finely chopped green onion

Preheat oven to 375 degrees. Place pie crust in a 9-inch pie plate and flute edges. Evenly sprinkle bacon bits and Swiss cheese in bottom of pie crust. In a blender container, combine eggs, flour, black pepper, nutmeg, evaporated milk, half & half, and onion. Cover and process on BLEND for 45 seconds. Pour mixture into pie crust. Bake for 40 to 45 minutes or until center is set. Place pie plate on a wire rack and let set for 5 minutes. Cut into 8 servings.

Each serving equals:

HE: 1 Bread • ¾ Protein • ½ Fat • ⅓ Fat-Free Milk • ¼ Slider • 5 Optional Calories

230 Calories • 10 gm Fat • 12 gm Protein • 23 gm Carbohydrate • 429 mg Sodium • 245 mg Calcium • 1 gm Fiber

DIABETIC EXCHANGES: 1½ Starch/Carbohydrate • 1 Meat • 1 Fat

Carrot Ring

This is just what it sounds like, a molded ring of cooked carrots flavored with just a bit of maple. This is a dish I'd expect to see on a menu in Massachusetts or Minnesota, a cold place where diners long to have their hearts warmed at the table! ☻ Serves 4

1 (16-ounce) can sliced carrots, rinsed and drained

1 tablespoon Log Cabin Sugar Free Maple Syrup

2 eggs or equivalent in egg substitute

1 tablespoon + 1 teaspoon I Can't Believe It's Not Butter! Light Margarine

2 slices reduced-calorie white bread, torn into small pieces

2 teaspoons dried onion flakes

⅛ teaspoon black pepper

Preheat oven to 375 degrees. Spray an 8-inch baking ring mold with butter-flavored cooking spray. In a blender container, combine carrots, maple syrup, and eggs. Cover and process on BLEND for 30 seconds. Add margarine, bread pieces, onion flakes, and black pepper. Re-cover and process on BLEND for 20 seconds or until mixture is smooth. Pour mixture into prepared ring mold. Bake for 25 to 30 minutes or until firm. Unmold onto serving plate. Cut into 4 servings.

HINTS: 1. Very attractive served with creamed peas in center.
2. If you don't have a ring mold, place washed empty carrot can in center of a pie plate and pour mixture around can in pie plate.

Each serving equals:

HE: 1 Vegetable • ½ Protein • ½ Fat • ¼ Bread • 2 Optional Calories

105 Calories • 5 gm Fat • 5 gm Protein • 10 gm Carbohydrate • 317 mg Sodium • 42 mg Calcium • 1 gm Fiber

DIABETIC EXCHANGES: 1 Vegetable • ½ Meat • ½ Fat

Creamy Corn Pudding

This dish puffs up so beautifully when you bake it, you'll want to save it for company meals—but don't. Your family will clamor for corn pudding often, and this is the best way to give them the flavor they crave without worrying about the fat in the classic version.

● Serves 6

> 3 eggs or equivalent in egg substitute
> 2 tablespoons I Can't Believe It's Not Butter! Light Margarine
> 1 tablespoon Splenda Granular
> 1 (12-fluid-ounce) can Carnation Evaporated Fat-Free Milk
> 3 tablespoons all-purpose flour
> 2½ cups frozen whole-kernel corn, thawed
> 2 teaspoons dried onion flakes
> ⅛ teaspoon black pepper

Preheat oven to 350 degrees. Spray an 8-by-8-inch baking dish with butter-flavored cooking spray. In a blender container, combine eggs, margarine, Splenda, and evaporated milk. Cover and process on BLEND for 60 seconds. Add flour, corn, onion flakes, and black pepper. Re-cover and process on BLEND for 15 seconds. Pour mixture into prepared baking dish. Bake for 1 hour or until center is firm. Place baking dish on a wire rack and let set for 5 minutes. Divide into 6 servings.

HINT: Thaw corn by placing in a colander and rinsing under hot
water for one minute.

Each serving equals:

HE: 1 Bread • ½ Fat-Free Milk • ½ Protein • ½ Fat •
1 Optional Calorie

197 Calories • 5 gm Fat • 10 gm Protein •
28 gm Carbohydrate • 160 mg Sodium •
177 mg Calcium • 2 gm Fiber

DIABETIC EXCHANGES: 1 Starch • ½ Fat-Free Milk •
½ Meat • ½ Fat

Spanish Rice Supreme

In restaurant kitchens, blenders are a mainstay for preparing rich sauces for all kinds of dishes, including this classic South of the Border pleaser. Does it surprise you that I'm even mixing the cheese into the blend? I discovered that it makes for an incredible flavor boost! ◐ Serves 6

1 (16-ounce) can tomatoes, undrained
1 (8-ounce) can Hunt's Tomato Sauce
1 cup coarsely chopped onion
1 cup coarsely chopped green bell pepper
1 (2-ounce) jar chopped pimiento, undrained
1 cup + 2 tablespoons (4½ ounces) shredded Kraft reduced-fat Cheddar cheese
1 tablespoon Splenda Granular
¼ teaspoon ground oregano
⅛ teaspoon black pepper
1 cup (3 ounces) uncooked Minute Rice

Preheat oven to 350 degrees. Spray an 8-by-8-inch baking dish with olive oil-flavored cooking spray. In a blender container, combine undrained tomatoes, tomato sauce, onion, and green pepper. Cover and process on BLEND for 30 seconds. Add undrained pimiento, Cheddar cheese, Splenda, oregano, and black pepper. Re-cover and process on BLEND for 15 seconds. Pour mixture into prepared baking dish. Add uncooked instant rice. Mix well to combine. Cover and bake for 30 minutes. Uncover and continue baking for 15 minutes or until rice is tender. Place baking dish on a wire rack and let set for 5 minutes. Divide into 6 servings.

Each serving equals:

HE: 2 Vegetable • 1 Protein • ½ Bread • 1 Optional Calorie

173 Calories • 5 gm Fat • 9 gm Protein • 23 gm Carbohydrate • 381 mg Sodium • 196 mg Calcium • 2 gm Fiber

DIABETIC EXCHANGES: 2 Vegetable • 1 Starch • 1 Meat

Dried Beef and Tomato Sauce over Toast

Sometimes the blender's best talent is taking ingredients with more texture than you want in your finished dish and smoo-oo-oothing them into something creamy and luscious. Here, the dried beef releases all of its intense taste into a satisfying sauce.

☻ Serves 4

> 1 (10¾-ounce) can Healthy Request Tomato Soup
> 1 (4.5-ounce) jar Armour 95% fat-free dried beef, rinsed and drained
> ¾ cup (3 ounces) shredded Kraft reduced-fat Cheddar cheese
> 2 teaspoons dried onion flakes
> 1 teaspoon dried parsley flakes
> 8 slices reduced-calorie bread, toasted

In a blender container, combine tomato soup, dried beef, Cheddar cheese, onion flakes, and parsley flakes. Cover and process on BLEND for 30 seconds. Pour mixture into a medium saucepan sprayed with butter-flavored cooking spray. Cook over medium heat until mixture is heated through and cheese is melted, stirring often. For each serving, place 2 slices of toast on a plate and spoon about ½ cup hot sauce over top.

Each serving equals:

HE: 1¾ Protein • 1 Bread • ½ Slider •
5 Optional Calories

263 Calories • 7 gm Fat • 18 gm Protein •
32 gm Carbohydrate • 983 mg Sodium •
199 mg Calcium • 1 gm Fiber

DIABETIC EXCHANGES: 1½ Meat •
1½ Starch/Carbohydrate

Banana Cream Pudding

Scrumptious, cool, and almost too creamy, this blender pudding concoction is downright dreamy! What a perfect end to a hearty meal, when you want sweetness that slides down your throat and reminds your tummy what a great meal you just ate.

☻ Serves 4

> 1 (12-fluid-ounce) can Carnation Evaporated Fat-Free Milk
> 2 cups (2 medium) diced bananas
> 2 teaspoons I Can't Believe It's Not Butter! Light Margarine
> 1 teaspoon vanilla extract
> 1 (4-serving) package JELL-O sugar-free vanilla cook-and-serve
>   pudding mix
> ¼ cup Cool Whip Lite

In a blender container, combine evaporated milk and bananas. Cover and process on BLEND for 15 seconds. Add margarine, vanilla extract, and dry pudding mix. Re-cover and process on BLEND for 15 seconds or until mixture is smooth. Pour mixture into a medium saucepan. Cook over medium heat until mixture thickens and starts to boil, stirring constantly using a wire whisk. Evenly spoon mixture into 4 dessert dishes. Cover and refrigerate for at least 1 hour. When serving, top each with 1 tablespoon Cool Whip Lite.

Each serving equals:

> HE: 1 Fruit • ¾ Fat-Free Milk • ¼ Fat • ¼ Slider •
> 10 Optional Calories
>
> ---
>
> 186 Calories • 2 gm Fat • 7 gm Protein •
> 35 gm Carbohydrate • 258 mg Sodium •
> 245 mg Calcium • 2 gm Fiber
>
> ---
>
> DIABETIC EXCHANGES: 1 Fruit • 1 Fat-Free Milk •
> ½ Starch/Carbohydrate

Chocolate Coconut Cream Pudding

I've always believed that the combination of chocolate and coconut is one of the greatest on earth, even before I tasted the classic candy bars that celebrate it. Now I leave those tasty-but-high-fat bars on the store shelf, instead luxuriating in this delightfully decadent dessert!   ☺   Serves 4

> 1 (4-serving) package JELL-O sugar-free chocolate cook-and-serve pudding mix
> 2 cups fat-free milk or soy milk
> ½ teaspoon coconut extract
> ¼ cup flaked coconut ☆
> ¼ cup Cool Whip Lite
> 1 tablespoon + 1 teaspoon mini chocolate chips

In a blender container, combine dry pudding mix, milk, and coconut extract. Cover and process on BLEND for 15 seconds. Pour mixture into a medium saucepan. Stir in 3 tablespoons coconut. Cook over medium heat until mixture thickens and starts to boil, stirring constantly using a wire whisk. Spoon hot mixture evenly into 4 dessert dishes. Refrigerate for at least 1 hour. When serving, top each with 1 tablespoon Cool Whip Lite and garnish with 1 teaspoon chocolate chips and ¾ teaspoon coconut.

Each serving equals:

HE: ½ Fat-Free Milk • ½ Slider • 12 Optional Calories

119 Calories • 3 gm Fat • 5 gm Protein •
18 gm Carbohydrate • 186 mg Sodium •
152 mg Calcium • 0 gm Fiber

DIABETIC EXCHANGES: ½ Fat-Free Milk • ½ Starch

Pumpkin Fluff Pie

I've listened to plenty of debates about pumpkin pie while traveling from one end of this nation to the other, but wherever I've gone, I've heard nothing but cheers for a lighter-than-air pie filling that transforms pumpkin into a dream dessert.   ☻   Serves 8

> 1 Pillsbury refrigerated unbaked 9-inch pie crust
> ½ cup Land O Lakes Fat Free Half & Half
> 2 eggs or equivalent in egg substitute
> 1 (15-ounce) can Libby's solid pack pumpkin
> ¾ cup Splenda Granular
> 1½ teaspoons pumpkin pie spice

Preheat oven to 400 degrees. Place pie crust in a deep-dish 9-inch pie plate and flute edges. In a blender container, combine half & half and eggs. Cover and process on BLEND for 15 seconds. Add pumpkin, Splenda, and pumpkin pie spice. Re-cover and process on BLEND for 30 seconds or until mixture is smooth stopping to stir as necessary. Pour mixture into unbaked pie crust. Bake for 45 to 50 minutes or until a knife inserted in center comes out clean. Place pie plate on a wire rack and allow to cool completely. Refrigerate for at least 30 minutes. Cut into 8 servings.

Each serving equals:

> HE: 1 Bread • ½ Fat • ½ Vegetable • ¼ Protein •
> 19 Optional Calories
> _____
> 168 Calories • 8 gm Fat • 3 gm Protein •
> 21 gm Carbohydrate • 133 mg Sodium •
> 46 mg Calcium • 2 gm Fiber
> _____
> DIABETIC EXCHANGES: 1½ Starch/Carbohydrate • 1 Fat

Grande Strawberry Pie

There's no better way to top a fresh strawberry pie filling than to blend more fresh strawberries into a sauce so superb it deserves a blue ribbon at the state fair! This saucy blend is so intensely strawberry, I smiled my way through every bite.   ☻   Serves 8

4 cups chopped fresh strawberries ☆
1 (6-ounce) Keebler graham cracker pie crust
1 cup Diet Mountain Dew
1 (4-serving) package JELL-O sugar-free vanilla cook-and-serve
    pudding mix
1 (4-serving) package JELL-O sugar-free strawberry gelatin
¼ teaspoon ground cinnamon
½ cup Cool Whip Lite

Evenly arrange 3 cups strawberries in pie crust. In a blender container, combine Diet Mountain Dew, remaining 1 cup strawberries, dry pudding mix, and dry gelatin. Cover and process on BLEND for 30 seconds or until mixture is smooth. Pour strawberry mixture into a medium saucepan. Stir in cinnamon. Cook over medium-low heat until mixture thickens and starts to boil, stirring constantly using a wire whisk. Place pie tin on a wire rack and pour hot mixture evenly over strawberries in pie crust. Let set for 5 minutes. Refrigerate for at least 2 hours. Cut into 8 servings. When serving, top each piece with 1 tablespoon Cool Whip Lite.

Each serving equals:

HE: 1 Bread • ½ Fruit • ¼ Fat • ¼ Slider •
5 Optional Calories

158 Calories • 6 gm Fat • 1 gm Protein •
25 gm Carbohydrate • 137 mg Sodium •
12 mg Calcium • 2 gm Fiber

DIABETIC EXCHANGES: 1 Starch • ½ Fruit • ½ Fat

Dutch Apple Crumb Pie

I decided to take an old-fashioned dessert that used to need lots of time to prepare properly, then transform it for busy cooks who love the spicy sweetness of apples and crumb topping. I think it lost nothing in the translation, don't you? ☻ Serves 8

3 cups (6 small) cored, peeled, and sliced cooking apples

1 (6-ounce) Keebler graham cracker pie crust

½ cup Land O Lakes Fat Free Half & Half

1 cup Splenda Granular

1 egg or equivalent in egg substitute

3 tablespoons all-purpose flour

1 teaspoon vanilla extract

1½ teaspoons apple pie spice

1 tablespoon + 1 teaspoon I Can't Believe It's Not Butter! Light Margarine

6 tablespoons purchased graham cracker crumbs or 2 (2½-inch) graham crackers, made into crumbs

¼ cup (1 ounce) coarsely chopped walnuts

Preheat oven to 350 degrees. Evenly arrange apple slices in pie crust. In a blender container, combine half & half, Splenda, egg, flour, vanilla extract, and apple pie spice. Cover and process on BLEND for 30 seconds. Pour mixture evenly over apples. In a medium bowl, combine margarine and graham cracker crumbs. Mix gently with a fork until it forms a crumbly mixture. Stir in walnuts. Evenly sprinkle crumb mixture over top. Bake for 50 to 55 minutes or until apples are tender. Place pie tin on a wire rack and allow to cool completely. Refrigerate for at least 30 minutes. Cut into 8 servings.

Each serving equals:

HE: 1½ Bread • 1 Fat • ¾ Fruit • ¼ Protein • ¼ Slider • 12 Optional Calories

225 Calories • 9 gm Fat • 4 gm Protein • 32 gm Carbohydrate • 189 mg Sodium • 60 mg Calcium • 2 gm Fiber

DIABETIC EXCHANGES: 1½ Starch/Carbohydrate • 1 Fat • 1 Fruit

Cherry Cream Cheese Pie

If you ever find yourself with less than an hour before dinner guests arrive, this is one scrumptious dessert you can whip up that is sure to win you some "oohs" and "aahs"! And oh, the gorgeous color just lights up the room. ◐ Serves 8

1 (8-ounce) package Philadelphia fat-free cream cheese, cubed
2 eggs or equivalent in egg substitute
¼ cup Splenda Granular
1 (6-ounce) Keebler graham cracker pie crust
½ teaspoon almond extract
1 (20-ounce) can Lucky Leaf No Sugar Added Cherry Pie Filling

Preheat oven to 325 degrees. In a blender container, combine cream cheese, eggs, and Splenda. Cover and process on BLEND for 30 seconds or until mixture is smooth. Pour mixture into pie crust. Bake for 20 minutes. Place pie tin on a wire rack and let set for 15 minutes. Stir almond extract into cherry pie filling. Evenly spread cherry pie filling over top of set filling. Refrigerate for at least 30 minutes. Cut into 8 servings.

Each serving equals:

HE: 1 Bread • ¾ Protein • ½ Fruit • ¼ Fat • 4 Optional Calories

178 Calories • 6 gm Fat • 7 gm Protein • 24 gm Carbohydrate • 300 mg Sodium • 86 mg Calcium • 2 gm Fiber

DIABETIC EXCHANGES: 1 Starch • ½ Meat • ½ Fruit • ½ Fat

Cherry Almond Cream Pie

I loved using my blender for this creamy dessert—I not only rested my whisking arm but also discovered that sometimes a machine is the perfect tool for creating the ultimate lush pie filling!

♥ Serves 8

1 Pillsbury refrigerated
    unbaked 9-inch
    pie crust
1 (20-ounce) can Lucky Leaf
    No Sugar Added Cherry
    Pie Filling
2 (8-ounce) packages
    Philadelphia fat-free
    cream cheese, cubed

2 eggs or equivalent in egg
    substitute
¾ cup Splenda Granular
1 teaspoon almond extract
½ cup Land O Lakes no-fat
    sour cream
½ cup Cool Whip Lite
2 tablespoons (½ ounce)
    slivered almonds

Preheat oven to 375 degrees. Place pie crust in 9-inch pie plate and flute edges. Spread cherry pie filling evenly in pie crust. Bake for 15 minutes. Meanwhile, in a blender container, combine cream cheese and eggs. Cover and process on CHOP for 30 seconds. Add Splenda and almond extract. Re-cover and process on CHOP for 30 seconds stopping to stir as necessary. Pour cream cheese mixture evenly over cherry filling. Bake for 30 minutes. Place pie plate on a wire rack and allow to cool completely. In a small bowl, gently combine sour cream and Cool Whip Lite. Spread mixture evenly over cooled pie and sprinkle almonds evenly over top. Refrigerate for at least 30 minutes. Cut into 8 servings.

Each serving equals:

HE: 1¼ Protein • 1 Bread • ¾ Fat • ½ Fruit •
¼ Slider • 18 Optional Calories

258 Calories • 10 gm Fat • 11 gm Protein •
31 gm Carbohydrate • 425 mg Sodium •
191 mg Calcium • 1 gm Fiber

DIABETIC EXCHANGES: 1½ Starch/Carbohydrate •
1 Meat • 1 Fat

Sour Cream Raisin Pecan Pie

This is my newest candidate for prizewinner at the potluck, so if you've got one coming up, consider this for your contribution! It's just so smoother-than-smooth, it's bound to be gobbled up faster than you can say thanks for all the applause. ☻ Serves 8

1 Pillsbury refrigerated unbaked 9-inch pie crust

2 eggs or equivalent in egg substitute

1 cup Land O Lakes no-fat sour cream

¾ cup Splenda Granular

1 teaspoon vanilla extract

1 cup seedless raisins

¼ cup (1 ounce) chopped pecans

Preheat oven to 350 degrees. Place pie crust in 9-inch pie plate and flute edges. In a blender container, combine eggs, sour cream, Splenda, and vanilla extract. Cover and process on BLEND for 20 seconds or until mixture is smooth. Add raisins and pecans. Re-cover and process on CHOP for 10 seconds. Pour mixture into pre-pared pie crust. Bake for 45 to 50 minutes or until filling is set. Place pie plate on a wire rack and allow to cool for 30 minutes. Refrigerate for at least 1 hour. Cut into 8 servings.

Each serving equals:

HE: 1 Bread • 1 Fruit • 1 Fat • ¼ Protein •
¼ Slider • 19 Optional Calories

246 Calories • 10 gm Fat • 4 gm Protein •
35 gm Carbohydrate • 158 mg Sodium •
57 mg Calcium • 1 gm Fiber

DIABETIC EXCHANGES: 1½ Starch/Carbohydrate •
1 Fruit • 1 Fat

No-Bake Blender Cheesecake

I've tasted cheesecakes from coast to coast, in tiny Mom-and-Pop restaurants and in fancy hotels. I think this is a terrific way to get the taste we all crave without devoting hours of prep time or risking your health to gobble down a high-fat version. ☻   Serves 8

½ cup boiling water

1 (4-serving) package JELL-O sugar-free lemon gelatin

2 tablespoons Diet Mountain Dew

2 cups fat-free cottage cheese

1½ cups Cool Whip Lite

1 (6-ounce) Keebler graham cracker pie crust

2 tablespoons purchased graham cracker crumbs or 2 (2½-inch)
graham crackers, made into crumbs

In a blender container, combine boiling water and dry gelatin. Cover and process on BLEND for 10 seconds or until gelatin is dissolved. Add Diet Mountain Dew and cottage cheese. Re-cover and process on BLEND for 30 seconds. Add Cool Whip Lite. Re-cover and process on BLEND for 15 seconds. Pour mixture into pie crust. Evenly sprinkle graham cracker crumbs over top. Refrigerate for at least 1 hour. Cut into 8 servings.

Each serving equals:

HE: 1 Bread • ½ Protein • ¼ Fat • ¼ Slider • 19 Optional Calories

---

166 Calories • 6 gm Fat • 8 gm Protein • 20 gm Carbohydrate • 336 mg Sodium • 40 mg Calcium • 1 gm Fiber

---

DIABETIC EXCHANGES: 1½ Starch/Carbohydrate • ½ Meat

Making Healthy Exchanges Work for You

You're ready now to begin a wonderful journey to better health. In the preceding pages, you've discovered the remarkable variety of good food available to you when you begin eating the Healthy Exchanges way. You've stocked your pantry and learned many of my food preparation "secrets" that will point you on the way to delicious success.

But before I let you go, I'd like to share a few tips that I've learned while traveling toward healthier eating habits. It took me a long time to learn how to eat *smarter*. In fact, I'm still working on it. But I am getting better. For years, I could *inhale* a five-course meal in five minutes flat—and still make room for a second helping of dessert!

Now I follow certain signposts on the road that help me stay on the right path. I hope these ideas will help point you in the right direction as well.

1. **Eat slowly** so your brain has time to catch up with your tummy. Cut and chew each bite slowly. Try putting your fork down between bites. Stop eating as soon as you feel full. Crumple your napkin and throw it on top of your plate so you don't continue to eat when you are no longer hungry.

2. **Smaller plates** may help you feel more satisfied by your food portions *and* limit the amount you can put on the plate.

3. **Watch portion size.** If you are *truly* hungry, you can always add more food to your plate once you've finished your initial serving. But remember to count the additional food accordingly.

4. **Always eat at your dining room or kitchen table.** You deserve better than nibbling from an open refrigerator or over the sink. Make an attractive place setting, even if you're eating alone. Feed your eyes as well as your stomach. By always eating at a table, you will become much more aware of your true food intake. For some reason, many of us conveniently "forget" the food we swallow while standing over the stove or munching in the car or on the run.

5. **Avoid doing anything else while you are eating.** If you read the paper or watch television while you eat, it's easy to consume too much food without realizing it, because you are concentrating on something else besides what you're eating. Then, when you look down at your plate and see that it's empty, you wonder where all the food went and why you still feel hungry.

Day by day, as you travel the path to good health, it will become easier to make the right choices, to eat *smarter*. But don't ever fool yourself into thinking that you'll be able to put your eating habits on cruise control and forget about them. Making a commitment to eat good healthy food and sticking to it takes some effort. But with all the good-tasting recipes in this Healthy Exchanges cookbook, just think how well you're going to eat—and enjoy it—from now on!

Healthy Lean Bon Appetit!

Index

I want to hear from you . . .

Besides my family, the love of my life is creating "common folk" healthy recipes and solving everyday cooking questions in *The Healthy Exchanges Way*. Everyone who uses my recipes is considered part of the Healthy Exchanges Family, so please write to me if you have any questions, comments, or suggestions. I will do my best to answer. With your support, I'll continue to stir up even more recipes and cooking tips for the Family in the years to come.

> Write to: JoAnna M. Lund
> c/o Healthy Exchanges, Inc.
> P.O. Box 80
> DeWitt, IA 52742-0080

If you prefer, you can fax me at 1-563-659-2126 or contact me via e-mail by writing to HealthyJo@aol.com. Or visit my Healthy Exchanges Internet web site at: http://www.healthyexchanges.com.

Now That You've Seen
Sensational Smoothies
Why Not Order
The Healthy Exchanges Food Newsletter?

If you enjoyed the recipes in this cookbook and would like to cook up even more of these "common folk" healthy dishes, you may want to subscribe to *The Healthy Exchanges Food Newsletter*.

This monthly 12-page newsletter contains 30-plus new recipes *every month* in such columns as:

- Reader Exchange
- Reader Requests
- Recipe Makeover
- Micro Corner
- Dinner for Two

- Crock Pot Luck
- Meatless Main Dishes
- Rise & Shine
- Our Small World

- Brown Bagging It
- Snack Attack
- Side Dishes
- Main Dishes
- Desserts

In addition to all the recipes, other regular features include:

- The Editor's Motivational Corner
- Dining Out Question & Answer
- Cooking Question & Answer
- New Product Alert
- Success Profiles of Winners in the Losing Game
- Exercise Advice from a Cardiac Rehab Specialist
- Nutrition Advice from a Registered Dietitian
- Positive Thought for the Month

The cost for a one-year (12-issue) subscription is $28.50. To order, call our toll-free number. We accept all major credit cards.

1-800-766-8961 for Customer Orders
1-563-659-8234 for Customer Service

Thank you for your order, and for choosing to become a part of the Healthy Exchanges Family!

About the Author

JoAnna M. Lund, a graduate of the University of Western Illinois, worked as a commercial insurance underwriter for eighteen years before starting her own business, Healthy Exchanges, Inc., which publishes cookbooks, a monthly newsletter, motivational booklets, and inspirational audiotapes. Healthy Exchanges Cookbooks have more than 1 million copies in print. A popular speaker with hospitals, support groups for heart patients and diabetics, and service and volunteer organizations, she has appeared on QVC, on hundreds of regional television and radio shows, and has been featured in newspapers and magazines across the country.

The recipient of numerous business awards, JoAnna was an Iowa delegate to the national White House Conference on Small Business. She is a member of the International Association of Culinary Professionals, the Society for Nutritional Education, and other professional publishing and marketing associations. She lives with her husband, Clifford, in DeWitt, Iowa.

HAVE YOU TRIED THESE HEALTHY EXCHANGES BOOKS?

Healthy Exchanges Cookbook   0-399-52554-8   *$13.95/$19.95 Can.*
The Diabetics Healthy Exchanges Cookbook   0-399-52235-2
    $14.00/$20.00 Can.
The Heart Smart Healthy Exchanges Cookbook   0-399-52474-6
    $14.00/$20.00 Can.
The Strong Bones Healthy Exchanges Cookbook   0-399-52337-5
    $13.95/$19.95 Can.
The Arthritis Healthy Exchanges Cookbook   0-399-52377-4
    $13.95/$19.95 Can.
Cooking Healthy with a Man in Mind   0-399-52779-6
    $16.95/$24.99 Can.
Cooking Healthy with the Kids in Mind   0-399-52605-6
    $13.95/$19.99 Can.
String of Pearls   0-399-52745-1   *$13.95/$19.99 Can.*
A Potful of Recipes   0-399-52650-1   *$15.95/$22.99 Can.*
The Open Road Cookbook   0-399-52862-8   *$17.95/$27.00 Can.*
The Healthy Exchanges Diabetic Desserts Cookbook   0-399-52884-9
    $17.95/$27.00 Can.

AVAILABLE WHEREVER BOOKS ARE SOLD